Spanish

verb handbook

Mike Zollo

Berlitz Publishing Company, Inc.

Princeton   Mexico City   London   Eschborn   Singapore

Spanish Verb Handbook

Copyright © 1993 Mike Zollo
Published by Berlitz Publishing Co., Inc.
400 Alexander Park, Princeton, NJ 08540 USA
9-13 Grosvenor St., London W1X 9FB UK

Reprinted January 2001
Printed in Canada
ISBN 2-8315-6397-6

The Author:
Mike Zollo is an experienced teacher, author and chief examiner. He is the chairman of the Association for Language Learning Spanish and Portuguese Committee.

Series Editor:
Christopher Wightwick is a former UK representative on the Council of Europe Modern Languages Project and Principal Inspector of Modern Languages for England.

Author's acknowledgment
I would like to thank Matilde Gutiérrez Manjón for her meticulous checking of the typescript and for some invaluable suggestions.

CONTENTS

How to Use This Handbook

This Handbook aims to provide a full description of the Spanish verb system for all learners and users of the Spanish language. It provides the following information:

• a chapter explaining the verb system in Spanish;

• the conjugation of fifty-eight verbs, grouped to show the common patterns underlying the system;

• a subject index to The Verb System in Spanish;

• a verb index, containing over twenty-two hundred verbs with their English meanings and references to the pattern(s) they follow.

An important feature of the book is that examples, showing many of the verbs in use, are given throughout The Verb System in Spanish and the Model Verbs.

THE VERB SYSTEM IN SPANISH

Use the Contents and Subject Index to find your way around this section, which describes the functions and forms of verbs in general. It provides information on the use of tenses, word order, the way verbs govern other parts of speech, and the way verbs are formed. It also describes methods of avoiding the passive, and it explains features such as the reflexive forms, the subjunctive, the verbs **ser** and **estar,** and the auxiliary verbs. It explains the main features of predictability and irregularity, and it illustrates key irregular verbs.

MODEL VERBS

Use the Verb Index to find your way around this section, which gives the full conjugation of one key model verb (**amar**) in all of its active and passive forms and of every tense of the other verbs in their active forms. This section provides models for all three groups of regular verbs plus the full range of spelling-change and stem-changing verbs, followed by all useful irregular verbs. This makes a total of fifty-eight model verbs.

The conjugation of each verb is given in all usable tenses. Tenses that have any irregularity are given in full. For tenses that are predictable, and most especially for compound tenses, only the first person singular form is given, as this is sufficient to enable you to predict the other forms within those tenses. Therefore, if a tense is not given in full, you can assume that it is regular.

For simple tenses, just look at the first model verb (**amar**) or at one of the three regular verb models (model verbs 2, 3, and 4) to figure out the endings needed. For compound tenses, check The Verb System in Spanish to decide which tense of which auxiliary verb is necessary, then look up the appropriate auxiliary verb (**haber, estar,** or **ser**) in the Model Verbs.

Where appropriate, the model verb pages also contain the following:

• A list of other verbs that follow the same pattern. If possible, all such verbs are given. If, however, they are too numerous to list, a selection of the most useful ones is given. There are, of course, verbs that stand alone, having no others following their model.

• Notes indicating the main features of this pattern and any variations or additional features affecting any of the verbs that basically follow that model.

• Short dialogues, narratives, or sentences that illustrate some of the different tenses and usages of these verbs.

For further information on how the verb system works, refer to The Verb System in Spanish.

SUBJECT INDEX

The Subject Index gives section references for all of the main grammatical terms used in The Verb System in Spanish.

VERB INDEX

For each of the twenty-two hundred or so verbs listed, the Verb Index gives information on whether it is transitive *(tr)*, intransitive *(intr)*, or reflexive *(refl)*, together with its English meaning. It also lists common secondary meanings and the main idiomatic expressions based on common verbs. Finally, each entry is referred to the model verb whose pattern it follows:

* **jugar (a)** (*intr*)   play; gamble   **21**

jugar el papel de (*intr*)   act out, play a role

There are verbs that have more than one predictable or unpredictable variation from the norm. Such verbs have two numbers after them, and both model verb pages should be consulted in these cases.

HOW TO FIND THE INFORMATION YOU WANT

If you want to check on the form, meaning, or use of a verb, look it up in the Verb Index. This shows:

• which verbs are model verbs (indicated by an asterisk);

* abrir (*tr/intr*) open, open up **25**

• any preposition normally accompanying the verb;

echar la culpa a (*tr*) blame **2**

• whether the verb is transitive (*tr*), intransitive (*intr*), or reflexive (*refl*);

acabar (*tr*) finish, complete **2**

• the main English meaning of the verb, along with any important idiomatic uses;

entregar (*tr*) deliver, hand over, hand in; turn over, yield **7**

entregarse a (*refl*) become addicted

• a number indicating the model verb, which gives the conjugation of the verb, points out its irregularities, and lists verbs.

absorber (*tr*) absorb **3**

A

THE VERB SYSTEM IN SPANISH

What Verbs Do

Note: For more extensive treatment of the functions and uses of Spanish verbs, see the Berlitz *Spanish Grammar Handbook.*

1a   Full Verbs

The great majority of verbs tell us about the action, state of mind, or (possibly changing) situation of the subject of the sentence. These are called *full* verbs.

Vivo en una granja.	*I live* on a farm.
Tenemos un perro.	*We have* a dog.

1b   Auxiliary Verbs

A much smaller group of verbs is used almost exclusively to add something to the sense of a full verb—for example, to make a compound tense or to add a comment on an action. These are called *auxiliary* (helping) verbs.

He comprado una casa.	*I have* bought a house.
Suelo ir a la oficina en coche.	*I usually* go to the office by car.

1c   Dual-Purpose Verbs

Some verbs can be used either with their full meanings or as auxiliaries. For example, the verb **estar** (to be)—used mostly to express the position or the state or the condition of something or somebody—is also used as the auxiliary verb to form the present progressive tense, which describes an action currently in progress.

Está en la cocina.	*She is* in the kitchen.
Está preparando la cena.	*She is* preparing dinner.

What Verbs Govern

A sentence can contain many items of information other than what is given by the subject and the main verb. Some of these items depend directly on the main verb and cannot be removed without leaving the sentence incomplete. These items are said to be *governed* by the verb.

2a   *Lone Verbs (Intransitive Verbs)*

Some verbs do not normally govern an object [➤2c], though the sentence may, of course, contain adverbials that add to the meaning. These verbs are called *intransitive verbs* and are usually marked in verb lists and dictionaries as (intr).

Estaban charlando ruidosamente.	*They were chatting* noisily.

They were chatting makes sense by itself. Although we know how they were chatting (noisily), this information is not necessary for the sentence to make sense.

2b   *Verbs Linking Equals: The Complement*

A small number of verbs simply act as links between the subject and another word or phrase, which is called the *complement* of the verb. Usually the complement is a noun phrase, referring to the same person or thing as the subject.

Mi padre fue *profesor*.	My father was *a teacher*.

It can be seen that the noun phrase complement (*a teacher*) refers to the subject (*my father*).

2c   *Verbs with One Object (Transitive Verbs)*

Many verbs take a *direct object* (i.e., the person or thing affected by the main verb). These verbs are *transitive*. They are usually marked in dictionaries and verb lists as (tr). A direct object answers the question *what?* or *whom?* Intransitive verbs cannot have a direct object.

Mi amigo compró *un perro*.	My friend bought *a dog*.

Here, *a dog* is what my friend bought, so it is the direct object of *bought*.

2d Verbs That Can Be Both Transitive and Intransitive

Many verbs can be used both transitively and intransitively in Spanish, either standing alone or having an object. They may be listed as (tr/intr) in verb lists and dictionaries.

Mis amigos *hablaban* mucho.	My friends *were talking* a lot.
***Ellos hablaban español*.**	*They were speaking Spanish.*

2e Verbs with Two Objects: Direct and Indirect

Some transitive verbs describe the transfer of the direct object to another person (or possibly thing). This person is then the *indirect object* of the verb. With some verbs the idea can be extended to include people indirectly affected by the action of the verb. The indirect object answers the question *to whom?* or *for whom?*

Siempre le da *diez pesetas al mendigo*.	He always gives *ten pesetas to the beggar*.

The money is the direct object, and the beggar—the beneficiary — is the indirect object.

2f Objects That Refer to the Subject: Reflexive Verbs

Another type of verb describes an action that 'rebounds' or 'reflects' on the subject; in other words, the subject and the indirect object are one and the same. In English, they will often involve the use of one of the '-self' pronouns. These are called *reflexive verbs*; the vast majority of these verbs can be used as ordinary transitive verbs too—e.g., **lavar** (to wash), **lavarse** (wash oneself). Many verbs are reflexive in Spanish but not in English.

Se está duchando.	*He's taking a shower.*
Todos los días, *se despertaba* temprano.	*Every day, he used to wake up early.*
***Se lavó* las manos antes de comer.**	*He washed his hands before eating.*

2g   *Verbs Plus Prepositions*

Many verbs, including those describing motion or situation, are supported by an adverb or a prepositional phrase.

Estamos *aquí*.	*We are here.*
Vive *en aquella casa*.	*He lives in that house.*

2h   *Verbs Governing Verbs*

(i)   *Verbs + infinitives*

This is a very common structure in Spanish. It has many expressions based on a modal auxiliary verb [➤3 below].

Queremos *salir* a las ocho.	*We want to go out at eight.*
Me gusta mucho *bailar*.	*I like dancing very much.*
¿Sabes *nadar*?	*Do you know how to swim?*

(ii)   *Verbs + prepositions + infinitives*

Spanish also has a number of these structures. They are very similar to the one above, but with a preposition between the auxiliary verb and the main verb.

Vamos *a cenar* en un restaurante.	*We are going to dine in a restaurant.*

Acababan de llegar.	*They had just arrived.*
Salió sin cerrar la puerta.	*She went out without shutting the door.*

(iii)   Verbs + participles

(A) Verb + present participle: Like English, Spanish has a way of describing an action in progress. This is done by using the verb **estar** (be) with the present participle of a verb, usually referred to by Spanish teachers as the *gerund.*

Estábamos comiendo cuando llegó.	*We were eating* when he arrived.

(B) Verb + past participle: Past events can be described by using the auxiliary verb **haber** with the past participle of a verb. In addition, **ser** plus the past participle of a verb is used to form the passive [➤9], and **estar** plus the past participle of a verb can be used to describe a state resulting from an action.

El capitán *ha llegado.*	The captain *has arrived.*
La nueva guía *será publicada* **en mayo.**	The new guide *will be published* in May.
La ventana *está rota.*	The window *is broken.*

2i   Position of Verbs in the Sentence

(i)   Generally speaking, the word order in a sentence in Spanish is similar to that of a sentence in English; if anything, word order in Spanish is slightly more flexible, but experience is more useful here than any hard-and-fast rules.

(ii)   One important difference is that verbs in Spanish are usually found without an accompanying subject pronoun [➤10a]. This is because each verb ending is clear and distinct, not only in the written, but also in the spoken form. The verb endings themselves, therefore, convey the idea of person without the need for subject pronouns. However, the pronouns are used for emphasis, contrast, or clarity, when necessary.

—¿Quién rompió la ventana?	"Who broke the window?"
—¡La rompió *él*, señor!	"*He* broke it, sir!"
—Bueno, *yo* voy al teatro y	So, *I*'m going to the theater, and
tú vas al cine, ¿no es así?	*you*'re going to the movies, right?
—¿Tiene *usted* coche?	Do *you* have a car?

(iii)   Questions

Questions in English are usually formed by inverting verb and subject (with or without the auxiliary *do*). However, in Spanish such inversion is both not very common and impossible to make unless there is a separate subject pronoun. Instead, questions are indicated by adding the inverted question mark at the beginning of the sentence in written Spanish, and by the question intonation pattern in spoken Spanish.

Mi madre tiene un coche nuevo.	My mother has a new car.
¿Tu madre tiene un coche nuevo?	
¿Tiene tu madre un coche nuevo?	Does your mother have a new car?
Tienes muchos amigos.	You have a lot of friends.
¿Tienes muchos amigos?	Do you have many friends?

(iv)   Negative expressions

Negative expressions in Spanish are quite straightforward and do not affect the position of the verb in the sentence. *No* and *not* are both translated by **no,** which is placed immediately before the verb and any dependent object pronouns.

Mi novio *no* va a la playa	My boyfriend is *not*
conmigo.	going to the beach with me.
—¿Lo tienes tú?	"Do you have it?"
—No, *no* lo tengo.	"No, I do*n't* have it."
—¿Has recibido la carta?	"Have you received the letter?"
—No, *no* la he recibido.	"No, I have*n't* received it."

No can be combined with other negative expressions (**nada, nunca, nadie,** etc.), which are usually placed around the verb.

No le dije *nada.*	I said *nothing* to him.
No fuimos *nunca* a Bogotá.	We *never* went to Bogota.

THE VERB SYSTEM IN SPANISH

No conocí a *nadie* en Las Vegas.	I did*n't* meet *anyone* in Las Vegas.

Note: **Nadie** (and sometimes **nada** and **nunca**) can begin a sentence, in which case there is no need for **no**. This does not affect the position of the verb in the sentence.

Nadie llama a la puerta.	There is *nobody* knocking at the door.
Nada se pudo recuperar.	*Nothing* could be recovered.
Nunca fuimos a Bogotá.	We *never* went to Bogota.

③ Attitudes to Action: Modal Verbs

3a The Function of Modal Verbs

Modal auxiliary verbs, as mentioned in 2h(i) above, modify full verbs to express additional viewpoints such as possibility, desire, and obligation. They are used in the appropriate persons and tenses, followed by the infinitives of the full verbs.

3b The Verbs and Their Meanings

The following are the main modal auxiliary verbs used in Spanish:

(i) *poder* be able to, can

No *puedo* ir contigo.	*I can't go with you*

(ii) *querer* want to, wish to

El testigo no *quería* decir más.	The witness *didn't want to* say anything else.

(iii) *gustar* please

This verb is used to express the idea of *liking*.

No *le gustaba* bailar.	He *didn't like* to dance.
¿*Te gustaría* salir conmigo?	*Would you like* to go out with me?

(iv) *deber* have to, must, be obliged to, ought to, should

¡No *debes* hacer eso!	*You must* not do that!
Deberían escuchar al profesor.	*They should/ought to* listen to the teacher.

THE VERB SYSTEM IN SPANISH

(v) **_deber de_** _must_

This verb is used to express probability.

Debe de **estar ya en Buenos Aires.**	_He must_ be in Buenos Aires by now.

(vi) **_tener que_** _have to, must, be obliged to_

Tenemos que **ir a casa.**	_We have to_ go home.

(vii) **_dejar_** _allow, permit_

Mis padres no me _dejarán_ salir.	My parents _will_ not _let_ me go out.

(viii) **_permitir_** _permit, allow_

No _se permite_ estacionar aquí.	Parking _is_ not _allowed_ here.

(ix) **_hacer_** _get something done, do, make_

Voy a _hacer_ reparar mi coche.	I'm going to _get_ my car fixed / repaired.

Note: **Gustar** and other verbs like it, such as **apetecer**, are known as impersonal or 'back-to-front' verbs. For more details on their use, see Berlitz _Spanish Grammar Handbook_.

Verb Forms Not Related to Time

Verbs are very versatile words, A verb form alone will usually tell you *who, what,* and *when* about the action/idea of the verb: *who* is responsible for it, *what* the action/idea is, *when* it takes place. However, there are some verb forms that do not specify the *who* or *when*.

4a The Infinitive

The key form of the verb, as found in a verb list or dictionary — and in the Verb Index of this book — is the *infinitive*, and this only explains *what* is being described. In Spanish, the infinitive form of all verbs ends in one of the following: **-ar, -er, -ir** (for example, **am*ar*, com*er*, viv*ir***).

4b The Two Participles

(i)   The present participle

This is a form of the verb often used to describe an action in progress; in Spanish, it is usually known as the *gerund*. The Spanish gerund form consists of the basic verb stem and the ending **-ando** (**-ar** verbs) or **-iendo** (**-er** and **-ir** verbs). Its most common use is with the auxiliary verb **estar,** to form the progressive tenses [➤6a(ii) and 6b(ii)]; but it can also be used by itself, provided that its subject and the subject of the other verb in the sentence are the same.

La chica está *dibujando* un gato.	The girl is *drawing* a cat.
Estaban *jugando* fútbol cuando los vi.	They were *playing* soccer when I saw them.
Cruzando la calle, vi un coche antiguo.	*Crossing* the street, I saw an old car.

Note: Although the present participle is often referred to as the *gerund* in Spanish, it is important not to confuse this term with the English gerund (the form that ends in '-ing'). The English gerund is often used in situations where Spanish uses an infinitive.

THE VERB SYSTEM IN SPANISH

| Me gusta *bailar*. | I like *dancing*. |
| Prohibido *fumar*. | No *smoking*. |

(ii)   The past participle

This form is used to describe an action that is finished. In Spanish, it ends in **-ado** (**-ar** verbs) or **-ido** (**-er** and **-ir** verbs). [➤6b(iv) for irregular past participles.] It is very often used with the auxiliary verb **haber** to form the perfect tenses and other compound tenses, but it is also used in other ways, including as an adjective and to form the passive. When used with **haber** in compound tenses, it does *not* need to agree with either the object or the subject, but elsewhere it does.

Ha *salido* sin decir nada.	He has *gone out* without saying anything.
Estos son los cuadros *pintados* por Picasso.	These are the pictures *painted* by Picasso.
En la calle había unas revistas *quemadas*.	In the street there were some *burnt* magazines.
Esta casa fue *construida* por mi padre.	This house was *built* by my father.

Note: The past participle is used as part of a compound tense in the first example above, as an adjective in the second and the third, and as part of a passive construction in the fourth.

In these last three examples, therefore, the past participles agree with the noun to which they relate, as it happens when the past participle is used as an adjective or is used to form the passive.

The Passage of Time and the Use of Tenses

5a What Do Tenses Tell Us?

Tenses are grammatical structures that often reflect a way of looking at an event as well as just recording when it takes place. Both the number of tenses and the denominations given to them vary from one language to another, though fortunately the main Spanish tenses correspond closely to those in English.

5b One Word or Two? Simple and Compound Tenses

Most verb forms consist of two parts. One describes *what* is going on; this basic part is called the *stem* or *root* of the verb, and for most tenses in Spanish it is the infinitive minus the **-ar, -er,** or **-ir** (for example, for the verbs **amar, comer,** and **vivir** these stems are **am-, com-,** and **viv-**). The other part defines *who* is responsible and *when* it is happening. There are two sorts of tenses: simple tenses and compound tenses.

(i) Simple tenses

These tenses are formed by adding special sets of endings to a basic stem or root: the stem tells *what* the action or idea is, and the ending gives the *who* and *when* information.

(ii) Compound tenses

These tenses use an auxiliary (helping) verb along with a special form of the main verb — a participle or the infinitive itself.

Thus, in the language of grammar, a simple tense is a one-word form, while a compound tense uses two or more words. Not counting the passive, in which all tenses are compound, Spanish has five simple tenses (seven including the subjunctive) and seven compound tenses (nine including the subjunctive). This is not as daunting as it seems, because some tenses are not used very often, especially in speech, and so it will probably be enough simply to be able to recognize them when you hear or read Spanish. In any case, once you know how to use the auxiliary verbs **haber, ser,** and **estar,** any compound tense can be formed by adding the appropriate participle.

13

THE VERB SYSTEM IN SPANISH

Note: In Spanish, the verb endings are clear and distinctive in both written and spoken language, and so subject pronouns (the person words listed in 10a below) are not usually needed, since the verb endings themselves make it *clear* who is involved [➤2i(ii)].

5c *Auxiliary Verbs Used to Form Compound Tenses*

In Spanish, the compound tenses fall into two groups, each using a different auxiliary verb. They should both prove easy for English speakers to master, as the positive forms are composed in exactly the same way as their equivalents in English.

(i) *The progressive tenses*

These tenses are used to describe actions that are in progress at the time being referred to. In English, they are easily identified, as they are formed by the appropriate form of the verb *be* followed by the main verb in the '-ing' form. Spanish uses an identical structure: the appropriate form of the verb **estar** followed by the *gerund* [➤4b(i)]. The two main tenses of this type are the present progressive and imperfect progressive: both describe an action in a more graphic, vivid way than their present and imperfect tense counterparts [➤6a(ii) and 6b(ii) below]. Note that Spanish uses the progressive tenses less than English, often preferring to use a simple tense.

¿No lo oyes? *Están llamando* **a la puerta.**	Can't you hear? *They are knocking* at the door.
Cuando me llamaste, *estaba planchando* **una camisa.**	When you called me *I was ironing* a shirt.

(ii) *The compound past tenses*

In English, these tenses are formed with the appropriate form of the verb *have*. Again, Spanish uses an identical structure: the appropriate form of the verb **haber** followed by the past participle.

Note: This is the only use of **haber** apart from the forms **hay, había,** etc., meaning *there is/are, there was/were,* etc. The verb **tener** is the verb normally used to convey the idea of possession.

¡*Ha llegado* **Manuel!**	Manuel *has arrived!*
***Habían visto* a Mariluz en la discoteca.**	*They had seen* Mariluz at the disco.

Note: The past participle is also used to form all passive forms [➤9 below].

Statements of Probable Fact: The Indicative

Verb forms and tenses that make a positive statement are said to be *indicative*. [Contrast this with the subjunctive: ➤8.]

In all verbs there are some tenses whose stems and endings can be predicted if you know one of the other parts of the verb. Parts that cannot be predicted in this way have to be learned, but once the principal parts are known, it is usually possible to predict other parts. It is helpful to know how to obtain the stem, to which the endings for each tense are added, and any spelling adjustments that may need to be made. The following sections give a breakdown of the main uses of each tense, and explain how to get the stem and endings for each tense, along with any pitfalls to watch out for.

6a   *The Present Tense*

In Spanish, the present tense can be used to convey the following ideas:

• What the situation is *now*.

En este momento mi amigo *habla* con el profesor de inglés.   At this moment my friend *is talking* to the English teacher.

• What happens *sometimes* or *usually*.

En casa, sólo *hablamos* español.   At home, *we* only *speak* Spanish.

• What is going to happen *(quite) soon*.

Mañana me *voy* a Caracas.   Tomorrow *I'm going* to Caracas.

• What has been happening *up to now* and may continue to happen.

Llevamos **diez minutos esperando.**	*We've been waiting* for ten minutes.
Estudio **español desde hace cuatro años.**	*I've been studying* Spanish for four years.

(i) *The present indicative*

This tense is formed by adding a set of endings to the stem of the verb, which consists of the infinitive with the **-ar, -er,** or **-ir** ending removed.

comprar *(buy)*	***comer*** *(eat)*	***vivir*** *(live)*
compr**o**	com**o**	viv**o**
compr**as**	com**es**	viv**es**
compr**a**	com**e**	viv**e**
compr**amos**	com**emos**	viv**imos**
compr**áis**	com**éis**	viv**ís**
compr**an**	com**en**	viv**en**

Be careful with all of the following [➤10b]:

• Spelling-change verbs with changes to the final consonant of their stem ➤10b(ii).
• Stem-changing verbs (all groups) ➤10b(v).
• Verbs whose first person singular stem ends in **-g-** (**poner,** etc.) ➤10b(vi).
• Verbs whose first person singular stem ends in **-zc-** (verbs ending in **-ocer, -ecer, -ucir**) ➤10b(vii).
• Verbs ending in **-uir** (**concluir,** etc.) ➤10b(iii).
• Verbs whose first person singular ending is **-oy** (**dar, estar, ir, ser**) ➤10b(viii).

For other irregular verbs, see Model Verbs.

(ii) *The present progressive*

This is formed by using the present tense of **estar** plus the *gerund* of the verb [➤4b(i)].

comprar → **comprando**   **comer** → **comiendo**   **vivir** → **viviendo**

Note: The following irregularities occur in the *gerund*:

• If the **-i-** of the ending comes between vowels, it becomes **-y-**: **leer** (*read*) → **leyendo, oír** (*hear*) → **oyendo,** and others [➤Model Verbs 12, 13].
• After **-ll-** and **-ñ-** the **-i-** is dropped: **zambullir** (*dive*) → **zambullendo, gruñir** (*grunt*) → **gruñendo.**
• The stressed vowel of the stem of some stem-changing verbs changes: **dormir** (*sleep*) → **durmiendo, vestir** (*dress*) → **vistiendo,** etc.

6b   *The Past Tenses*

(i)   *The imperfect indicative*

This tense is used for:
• repeated or habitual actions in the past;
• descriptions of things or people in the past;
• ongoing actions in the past, often as settings or backgrounds to other actions.

Iba a La Habana todos los años.	*He used to go* to Havana every year.
Era una casa muy grande.	*It was* a very big house.
Escribía una carta cuando entré.	*He was writing* a letter when I came in.

The imperfect indicative is formed by removing the infinitive ending and adding endings as follows:

comprar	*comer*	*vivir*
compr**aba**	com**ía**	viv**ía**
compr**abas**	com**ías**	viv**ías**
compr**aba**	com**ía**	viv**ía**
compr**ábamos**	com**íamos**	viv**íamos**
compr**abais**	com**íais**	viv**íais**
compr**aban**	com**ían**	viv**ían**

Note: The following verbs are irregular in the imperfect:

ser (be)	*Ir* (go)
era	iba
eras	ibas
era	iba
éramos	íbamos
erais	ibais
eran	iban

Ver (*see*) retains the **-e-**: **veía**, etc.

(ii)   *The imperfect progressive*

This tense is often used when a more vivid description of an ongoing action is needed. It is formed by using the appropriate imperfect tense form of **estar** followed by the *gerund* [➤5c(i) and compare ➤6a(ii)].

THE VERB SYSTEM IN SPANISH

Cuando llegaste, *yo estaba durmiendo.*   When you arrived, *I was sleeping.*

(iii) The preterite

This tense is used for a single, completed action in the past, even if it spanned a long period, as long as the precise amount of time is defined.

Compraron este terreno el año pasado.   *They bought* this land last year.

Vivió unos veinte años en Caracas.   *She lived* for about twenty years in Caracas.

The preterite is formed by removing the infinitive ending and adding the endings shown below. Note the stressed endings in the first and third persons singular.

comprar	*comer*	*vivir*
compré	comí	viví
compraste	comiste	viviste
compró	comió	vivió
compramos	comimos	vivimos
comprasteis	comisteis	vivisteis
compraron	comieron	vivieron

Note: Watch out for the **pretérito grave** [➤10b(ix)], where the ending of the first and third persons singular is not stressed and the stem can be irregular. Verbs of this type are marked *(pg)* in the Model Verbs. They include some very common verbs (**querer, tener, decir, poder,** etc.).

tener (have)	*decir* (say)
tuve	dije
tuviste	dijiste
tuvo	dijo
tuvimos	dijimos
tuvisteis	dijisteis
tuvieron	dijeron

There are further irregularities in the following types of verb, which should be checked in the relevant paragraph or section:
• Stem-changing verbs [➤10b(v)], types 2 and 3.
• Spelling-change verbs [➤10b(ii)].
• **Dar, ir, ser** [➤Model Verbs].

• Verbs where the third person plural ending (**-ieron**) follows a vowel, **-ll-**, or **-ñ-** [➤Model Verbs].

(iv) The rest of the past tenses in Spanish are compound tenses. They are formed using the appropriate tense of the auxiliary verb **haber** [➤Model Verbs] and the past participle [➤4b (ii) and 6b(v)]. Note the following irregular past participles:

abrir (open)	**abierto**
cubrir (cover)	**cubierto**
descubrir (discover, uncover)	**descubierto**
decir (say, tell)	**dicho**
disolver (dissolve)	**disuelto**
escribir (write)	**escrito**
freír (fry)	**frito**
hacer (make, do)	**hecho**
poner (put)	**puesto**
resolver (solve, resolve)	**resuelto**
romper (break)	**roto**
ver (see)	**visto**
volver (turn, return)	**vuelto**

Note: Compounds of these verbs have past participles with the same irregularities.

(v) The past participle is used with the appropriate tense of the auxiliary verb **haber** to form the following compound tenses, which largely correspond to their English equivalents.

(A) Present perfect tense (present of **haber** + past participle) The present perfect tense is usually used to refer to an action that has recently taken place, much as in English, though the preterite tense can be used in much the same way.

Hemos terminado el trabajo.   *We have finished* the work.

(B) Pluperfect tense (imperfect of **haber** + past participle) The pluperfect tense is used to take an extra step back from a time already in the past, which is the focus of attention. It corresponds to the English *had* + past participle.

Lo *habían visto* antes.   *They had seen* him before.

(C) Past anterior tense (preterite of **haber** + past participle)
The past anterior tense has the same meaning as the pluperfect, i.e., describing an action that *had taken place when*. . . . It is used instead of the pluperfect after certain expressions and is fairly rare. See the Berlitz *Spanish Grammar Handbook* for further explanation.

Antes de que *hube salido,* llegó a casa.	Before *I went out*, he arrived home.

(D) Future perfect tense (future of **haber** + past participle)
The future perfect tense is used to take a step forward from a time in the past to express the idea of *will have* + past participle.

***Habrá comido* ya, y no querrá nada más.**	*He will* already *have eaten* and won't want anything else.

(E) Conditional perfect tense (conditional of **haber** + past participle)
The conditional perfect tense is used to convey the idea of *would have*. . . , and is often used to express something hypothetical or unfulfilled.

***Habríamos tomado el sol,* pero llovía.**	*We would have sunbathed,* but it was raining.

6c The Future Tense

In Spanish, the future can be conveyed in one of two ways: the *future immediate* and the *future simple*.

(i) The future immediate

This describes an action about to happen. It is formed by the appropriate form of the verb **ir** plus **a** plus the infinitive of the verb. The structure is very similar to its equivalent in English.

***Vamos a nadar* en el mar.**	*We are going to swim* in the sea.
El jefe *va a volver* mañana.	The boss *is going to return* tomorrow.

(ii) The future simple

This is used for the following:

• Actions that are expected to happen in the future.

La semana que viene, _iremos_ a Valparaíso.   Next week _we'll go_ to Valparaiso.

• To express instructions.

Después de comer, _lavarás_ los platos, ¿no?   After eating, _you'll wash_ the dishes, won't you?

• To express predictions.

Lloverá esta tarde.   _It will rain_ this afternoon.

• To express probability.

Tendrá unos sesenta años.   _He's probably_ about sixty.

The future simple is formed by adding the appropriate set of endings to the _whole of the infinitive_. The only possible irregularity is in the stem, which always ends in **-r-** (see the irregular stems below). The endings are the same for all verbs. Note the stress accent on all the endings except **-emos.**

comprar	comer	vivir
comprar**é**	comer**é**	vivir**é**
comprar**ás**	comer**ás**	vivir**ás**
comprar**á**	comer**á**	vivir**á**
comprar**emos**	comer**emos**	vivir**emos**
comprar**éis**	comer**éis**	vivir**éis**
comprar**án**	comer**án**	vivir**án**

Note: The stems of the following verbs are irregular:

caber (fit)	**cabré**
decir (say)	**diré**
haber (have)	**habré**
hacer (do, make)	**haré**
poder (be able)	**podré**
poner (put)	**pondré**

querer (want, love)	**querré**
saber (know)	**sabré**
tener (have)	**tendré**
valer (be worth)	**valdré**
venir (come)	**vendré**

The compounds of any of these verbs have the same irregularities [➤10c].

6d The (Present) Conditional: What If?

Commonly referred to as 'the conditional,' the present conditional tense is used—broadly speaking—as the equivalent of *would* or *should* in English (but not necessarily with the sense of obligation). In the actual expression of conditions, it is used to indicate the outcome rather than the condition itself. It can also be used to express probability and the future in the past.

Me gustaría comprarlos.	*I'd like to buy them.*
Si tuviera dinero, *viviría* en San Francisco.	If he had the money, *he'd live* in San Francisco.
***Tendría* unos diez años cuando la vi por última vez.**	*She would have been* about ten the last time I saw her.
Dijo que después de llegar, *llamaría* a su madre.	He said that after arriving *he would call* his mother.

The (present) conditional has the same stem as the future tense [➤6c]. The endings are the same as the **-er/-ir** imperfect endings [➤6b(i)].

comprar	*comer*	*vivir*
comprar**ía**	comer**ía**	vivir**ía**
comprar**ías**	comer**ías**	vivir**ías**
comprar**ía**	comer**ía**	vivir**ía**
comprar**íamos**	comer**íamos**	vivir**íamos**
comprar**íais**	comer**íais**	vivir**íais**
comprar**ían**	comer**ían**	vivir**ían**

Note: The irregular stems in 6c also apply to the (present) conditional.

Requests and Commands: The Imperative

Orders and instructions can be given in a variety of ways:

• Expressing obligations.

***Tienes que* limpiar tu cuarto.**	*You have to* clean your room.

• Using the infinitive.

***Lavar* bien la fruta antes de comerla.**	*Wash* fruit well before eating it.

• Using the imperative forms of the verb, as detailed below.

7a The Informal Imperative Positive Singular

The informal imperative positive singular (the **tú** form) is formed by removing the final **-s** from the second person singular form of the present indicative tense.

compras → **compra**   comes → **come**   vives → **vive**

Note: The following verbs have irregular imperative forms:

decir	**di**	salir	**sal**
hacer	**haz**	ser	**sé**
ir	**ve**	tener	**ten**
poner	**pon**	venir	**ven**

¡*Compra* el mejor vino de España!	*Buy* the best wine of Spain!
¡*Sal* de ahí en seguida!	*Get out* of there at once!

Note also that pronouns can be attached to the end of positive imperatives. In that case, a written accent may be necessary to maintain the correct stress.

Dímelo.	Tell it to me.

7b   The Informal Imperative Positive Plural

The informal imperative positive plural (the **vosotros** form) is formed by removing the **-r** of the infinitive and adding **-d**. This is one of three instances where the endings of **-er** and **-ir** verbs differ—the first and second person plural of the present indicative being the other two [➤10b(i)]. Note that the **-d** drops out when the reflexive pronoun **-os** is added.

comprar	compra**d**	lavar(se)	lava**os**
comer	come**d**	poner(se)	pone**os**
vivir	vivi**d**	divertir(se)	divert**íos**

Note: • An accent is added on **-í-** when **-os** is added.

• The informal imperative positive plural for **irse** is **idos** (go away).

• The **vosotros** form is considered informal in Spain, but in most Latin American countries it is considered rather formal and is used in a limited manner. The alternative second person plural form, **ustedes,** is widely used for both formal and informal situations in the Latin American region.

***Comed* y *bebed* todo.**	*Eat* and *drink* it all.
***Ponedlos* en la mesa.**	*Put them* on the table.
***Sentaos*, chicos.**	*Sit down*, boys.

7c   Negative Informal Imperatives and All Formal Imperatives

The negative informal (**tú** and **vosotros**) and the positive formal (**usted** and **ustedes**) imperatives are formed in the same way as—or are the same as—their corresponding present subjunctive forms. Note that in the negative imperatives the object pronouns come immediately before the verb.

Informal negative

no compr**es**	no com**as**	no viv**as**
no compr**éis**	no com**áis**	no viv**áis**
no te lav**es**	no te pon**gas**	no te diviert**as**
no os lav**éis**	no os pon**gáis**	no os divirt**áis**

Formal positive

compre	coma	viva
compren	coman	vivan

Formal negative

no compre	no coma	no viva
no compren	no coman	no vivan
no se lave	no se ponga	no se divierta
no se laven	no se pongan	no se diviertan

Any irregularity in the present subjunctive tense will, of course, occur in these imperatives as well [▶8].

Vuelvan mañana.	*Come back* tomorrow.
Póngase este sombrero.	*Put* this hat *on.*
Llévenlos a casa.	*Take them* home.
¡No *te caigas!*	*Don't fall!*
No las *comáis.*	*Don't eat* them.
¡No me *miren* así!	*Don't look at* me like that!
No se *sienten* allí.	*Don't sit* there.
No las *compre.*	*Don't buy* them.

7d Summary of Imperative Forms

	Informal		Formal
Positive singular	compra	singular	compre
(tú)	come	(usted)	coma
	vive		viva
plural	comprad	plural	compren
(vosotros)	comed	(ustedes)	coman
	vivid		vivan
Negative singular	no compres	singular	no compre
(tú)	no comas	(usted)	no coma
	no vivas		no viva
plural	no compréis	plural	no compren
(vosotros)	no comáis	(ustedes)	no coman
	no viváis		no vivan

Areas of Uncertainty: The Subjunctive

The subjunctive is used whenever a less-than-fact statement is made; it can be a case of doubt or uncertainty, or a case of unfulfilled or hypothetical action. For more detailed explanation, see the Berlitz *Spanish Grammar Handbook.*

8a   *The Present Subjunctive*

Stem: Remove ending from the first person singular form of the present indicative tense.
Endings: Invert the order given for the indicative endings, i.e., for **-ar** verbs use the endings that begin with **-e-,** and for **-er** and **-ir** verbs use the endings that begin with **-a-.**

comprar	*comer*	*vivir*
compr**e**	com**a**	viv**a**
compr**es**	com**as**	viv**as**
compr**e**	com**a**	viv**a**
compr**emos**	com**amos**	viv**amos**
compr**éis**	com**áis**	viv**áis**
compr**en**	com**an**	viv**an**

Note: Watch out for the following:

• Stem-changing verbs of all types [➤10b(v)]. Pay particular attention to the further **e → i** and **o → u** changes in the second and third persons plural forms, types 2 and 3.
• Spelling changes in the final consonant of the stem [➤10b(ii)].
• Stems ending in **-g- (poner,** etc.) [➤10b(vi)].
• Stems with **-zc-** (verbs ending in **-ocer, -ecer, -ucir**) [➤10b(vii)].
• Verbs ending in **-uir (concluir,** etc.) [➤10b(iii)].

• Irregular present subjunctives: **caber → quepa, haber → haya, ir → vaya, saber → sepa, ser → sea.** (For full sets of forms, see the Model Verbs.)

No quiero que *comas* **eso.**	I don't want you to *eat* that.
Cuando *lleguemos,* **tomaremos un café.**	We'll have a coffee when *we arrive.*

8b   The Imperfect Subjunctive

Stem: Remove the ending from the third person plural form of the preterite tense.

Endings: There are two forms of this tense, which are totally interchangeable except that the **-ra** forms alone can be used to replace the conditional. (See the Berlitz *Spanish Grammar Handbook* for detailed explanation.)

-ra forms

comprara	comiera	viviera
compraras	comieras	vivieras
comprara	comiera	viviera
compráramos	comiéramos	viviéramos
comprarais	comierais	vivierais
compraran	comieran	vivieran

-se forms

comprase	comiese	viviese
comprases	comieses	vivieses
comprase	comiese	viviese
comprásemos	comiésemos	viviésemos
compraseis	comieseis	vivieseis
comprasen	comiesen	viviesen

Any of the stem irregularities that occur in the preterite tense [➤6b(iii)] are carried right through both forms of the imperfect subjunctive.

mentir (lie)	**mintieron**	**mintiera/mintiese**
dormir (sleep)	**durmieron**	**durmiera/durmiese**
leer (read)	**leyeron**	**leyera/leyese**
decir (say)	**dijeron**	**dijera/dijese**
ir/ser (go/be)	**fueron**	**fuera/fuese**

Si *fuera* rico, me compraría un Ferrari.   If *I were* rich, I'd buy a Ferrari.
Les dijo que *se callasen*.   He told them to *shut up*.

8c   Compound Subjunctive Tenses

The compound subjunctive tenses are formed by using the appropriate subjunctive tense of the auxiliary verb **haber** followed by the past participle of the main verb, as can be seen clearly in the Model Verbs [➤6b(iv) and 6b(v)].

⑨ Things Done to You: The Passive

9a The True Passive

Used to express an action from the point of view of the person or thing undergoing the action, the true passive is formed in Spanish in the same way as in English: use the appropriate form of the verb **ser** (be) followed by the past participle of the verb. (See Model Verbs for the complete conjugation of **ser**.) The only other thing to remember is that the past participle has to agree in gender and number with the subject, as in the following examples.

La ventana *fue rota* por ese chico.	The window *was broken* by that boy.
Ramón *fue atropellado* por un camión.	Ramón *was run over* by a truck/lorry.
Mis hermanas *han sido contratadas* por una compañía grande.	My sisters *have been hired* by a big company.

9b Alternatives to the True Passive

There are several ways of avoiding the true passive:

• Use the third person plural form of the verb impersonally.

Me dijeron que va a llover.	*I was told (they told me)* that it is going to rain.
Los robaron ayer.	*They were stolen (someone stole them)* yesterday.

• Invert the sentence if there is an agent that you can turn into the subject.

Lo mataron *los moros.*	He was killed by *the Moors* (*the Moors* killed him).

• Make the verb reflexive (this can only be done when the subject is inanimate).

28

La puerta *se cerró*.	The door *was closed* (*literally*: The door *closed itself*).
***Se cultiva* el arroz en la región de Valencia.**	Rice *is grown* (*literally: grows itself*) in the Valencia region.

• Use the redundant object pronoun.

La blusa *la* compró mi madre.	The blouse was bought by my mother (*literally*: The blouse — my mother bought *it*).

Types of Verb in Spanish

10a Predictability

The whole set of a verb's forms, including all tense forms, is known as its *conjugation*. Within each tense in Spanish, there are six different forms of the verb, each one corresponding to a particular person as follows:

first person singular:	**yo**	I
second person singular:	**tú**	you (familiar)
	usted	you (formal)
third person singular:	**él**	he
	ella	she
first person plural:	**nosotros/as**	we
second person plural:	**vosotros/as**	you (familiar plural)
	ustedes	you (formal plural)
third person plural:	**ellos**	they (masculine)
	ellas	they (feminine)

Note: *He, she*, and *you* (formal singular) share the same verb forms: *they* and *you* (formal plural) share the same verb forms.

The various parts of the set of verb forms, or conjugation, are *predictable* at several levels.

(i) Regular verbs

Regular verbs are those for which you can predict any form of any tense from the spelling of the infinitive (plus, of course, a knowledge of the rules!). Infinitives in Spanish end in **-ar, -er,** or **-ir** [▶4a], corresponding to the three main families of regular verbs, each with its own sets of forms and rules. Verbs for which some forms cannot be predicted in this way are *irregular*. Some of the most common Spanish verbs are irregular.

(ii) Imports

Verbs brought into Spanish from other languages and newly coined verbs tend to be regular **-ar** type of verbs.

dopar	dope, drug
esnifar	sniff (cocaine)
filmar	film

(iii)   *Irregular verbs*

Some irregular verbs have the same irregularities, so if you know one you can predict the forms of any of the others of that group. The so-called stem-changing verbs in Spanish fall into this category (**pensar, volver, pedir**, etc.).

There are also the following groups:

• those verbs that have a **-g-** in the first person singular form of the present indicative tense, and therefore throughout the present subjunctive (e.g., **pongo**);
• verbs with **-zc-** in the same place (e.g., **conozco**), and therefore throughout the present subjunctive;
• verbs with the irregular **pretérito grave** [▶10b(ix)].

(iv)   *Compound verbs*

With very few exceptions, compound verbs [▶10c] conjugate like their parent or base verb. Thus, for example, **contener, detener, mantener, obtener, retener, sostener** all behave as their parent verb **tener**.

10b   ***Major Groups of Verbs: How Are They Conjugated?***

(i)   *Conjugations*

There are three *conjugations* or groups of verbs in Spanish, which take a set of endings according to their infinitives [▶4a]. The infinitives end in **-ar, -er,** or **-ir;** and the regular or predictable members of each family [▶10a] behave in the same way, having the same sets of verb endings and methods of forming each tense. In fact, a look at the verb tables [▶The Complete System of Tenses in Spanish (Section B)] will show that throughout the whole range of tenses, the endings for **-er** and **-ir** verbs are identical except for the following three endings, which differ only in the vowel contained in the ending:

-er verbs (e.g., **comer**)
present indicative: **comemos, coméis**
familiar plural imperative: **comed**

-ir verbs (e.g., **vivir**)
present indicative: **vivimos, vivís**
familiar plural imperative: **vivid**

For the other tenses and persons, they have identical endings.

THE VERB SYSTEM IN SPANISH

(ii)   Spelling-change verbs

These are verbs whose spelling has to be adjusted to maintain the correct consonant sound with some endings. Therefore this applies only to the written language, and it affects the last consonant(s) of the stem. The changes fall into the following main categories:

-ar verbs: The following changes are necessary before **-e-** throughout the present subjunctive tense, and in the first person singular form of the preterite tense.
• Stem ends in **-c-** → **-qu-**.
sacar (take out): **saque, saques,** etc.; **saqué**
• Stem ends in **-z-** → **-c-**.
empezar (begin): **empiece, empieces,** etc.; **empecé**
• Stem ends in **-g-** → **-gu-**.
pagar (pay): **pague, pagues,** etc.; **pagué**
• Stem ends in **-gu-** → **-gü-**.
averiguar (verify): **averigüe, averigües,** etc.; **averigüé**

-er and **-ir** verbs: The following changes are necessary before **-o** in the first person singular form of the present indicative tense and before **-a-** throughout the present subjunctive tense.
• Stem ends in **-gu-** → **-g-**.
seguir (follow): **sigo; siga, sigas,** etc.
• Stem ends in **-g-** → **-j-**.
escoger (choose): **escojo; escoja, escojas,** etc.
• Stem ends in **-c-** → **-z-**.
torcer (twist): **tuerzo; tuerza, tuerzas,** etc.

(iii)   -uir verbs

Verbs ending in **-uir** have a **-y-** in the singular and third person plural forms of the present indicative tense, throughout the present and imperfect subjunctive tenses, in the third person form of the preterite tense (singular and plural), and in the gerund.

concluir (conclude)

present indicative:	**concluyo, concluyes, concluye, concluimos, concluís, concluyen**
present subjunctive:	**concluya, concluyas, concluya, concluyamos, concluyáis, concluyan**
preterite:	**concluí, concluiste, concluyó, concluimos, concluisteis, concluyeron**
imperfect subjunctive:	**concluyera / concluyese**
gerund:	**concluyendo**

(iv) *Accents*

A small number of verbs with their stems ending in **-i-** or **-u-** need an accent to stress this vowel in the singular and third person plural forms of the present tense.

enviar (send)
present indicative: **envío, envías, envía, enviamos, enviáis, envían**
present subjunctive: **envíe, envíes, envíe, enviemos, enviéis, envíen**

actuar (act)
present indicative: **actúo, actúas, actúa, actuamos, actuáls, actúan**
present subjunctive: **actúe, actúes, actúe, actuemos, actuéis, actúen**

Note: **Desviar** (divert), **situar** (situate), **graduar** (grade), and **continuar** (continue) follow the same rules.

(v) *Stem-changing verbs*

The biggest group of not quite regular, but predictably irregular verbs in Spanish are those that are variously known as radical-changing, root-changing, or stem-changing. In this book we refer to the part of the verb to which endings are added as the stem, so we shall use the term *stem-changing*.

You probably have noticed that many words in Spanish contain the diphthong **-ue-** or **-ie-,** where related words in English simply have **-o-** or **-e-**.

Spanish	*English*
puerto	port
muerto	mortuary
siete	septet
viento	ventilation

This stem change often happens in Spanish when in a conjugation, the syllable of the stem containing the original **-e-, -o-,** or **-u-** is stressed. When a verb is conjugated, the stress varies from stem to ending according to the person and tense, and in some verbs the stem changes when stressed.

There are three main types of stem-changing verbs:

Type 1: **-ar** and **-er** verbs
Stem change: **e** to **ie, o** to **ue,** and **u** to **ue** (**jugar** only).
The changes occur only in the present indicative and subjunctive tenses, where the stem is stressed, i.e., in all three singular forms and the third person plural form.

pensar (think)
present indicative: **pienso, piensas, piensa, piensan**
present subjunctive: **piense, pienses, piense, piensen**

volver (turn, return)
present indicative: **vuelvo, vuelves, vuelve, vuelven**
present subjunctive: **vuelva, vuelvas, vuelva, vuelvan**

jugar (play)
present indicative: **juego, juegas, juega, juegan**
present subjunctive: **juegue, juegues, juegue, jueguen**

> Type 2: **-ir** verbs
> Verbs of this type, like **mentir** (lie) or **dormir** (sleep), have the *same changes* in the *same places* as those of type 1. In addition, the stem vowel changes from **e** to **i** and **o** to **u** in the following tenses:

gerund: **mintiendo, durmiendo** [▶4b(i)]
present subjunctive: the first and second person plural forms [▶8a]
    mintamos, mintáis; durmamos, durmáis
preterite: the third person singular and plural forms [▶6b(iii)]
    mintió, mintieron; durmió, durmieron
imperfect subjunctive: throughout both forms of this tense [▶8b]
    mintiera/mintiese; durmiera/durmiese

> Type 3: **-ir** verbs
>
> Verbs of this type have the stem change in all the same places as type 2, but the change is *always* **e** to **i**.

pedir (request, ask for)
present indicative: **pido, pides, pide, piden**
present subjunctive: **pida, pidas, pida, pidamos, pidáis, pidan**
gerund: **pidiendo**
preterite: **pidió, pidieron**
imperfect subjunctive: **pidiera/pidiese**

(vi)   *-g- verbs*

> There is a group of verbs in which the stem of the present indicative contains **-g-** in the first person singular form only, and therefore throughout the present subjunctive tense. Some have a perfectly regular present indicative tense except for the first person form; others have stem changes [▶10b(v)].

hacer (do, make)
present indicative: **hago, haces, hace, hacemos, hacéis, hacen**
present subjunctive: **haga, hagas, haga, hagamos, hagáis, hagan**

tener (have)
present indicative: **tengo, tienes, tiene, tenemos, tenéis, tienen**
present subjunctive: **tenga, tengas, tenga, tengamos, tengáis, tengan**

The following verbs follow the same pattern:

caer (fall):   **caigo, caes,** etc.
poner (put):   **pongo, pones,** etc.
salir (go out):   **salgo, sales,** etc.
valer (be worth):   **valgo, vales,** etc.
decir (say):   **digo, dices, dice, decimos, decís, dicen**
oír (hear):   **olgo, oyes, oye, oímos, oís, oyen**

Note: Both the otherwise regular verbs and the stem-changing verbs keep the **-g-** stem unchanged throughout the present subjunctive.

(vii)   *-zc- verbs*

Another sizable group with an irregular first person singular form in the present indicative tense consists of verbs whose infinitives end in **-ecer, -ocer,** and **-ucir.** The stem of the first person form of the present indicative tense — and therefore all of the present subjunctive tense — ends in **-zc-.**

parecer (seem)
present indicative: **parezco, pareces, parece, parecemos, parecéis, parecen**
present subjunctive: **parezca, parezcas, parezca, parezcamos, parezcáis, parezcan**

The following verbs follow the same pattern, just as many other verbs ending in **-ecer** and all other verbs ending in **-ducir** do:

conocer	know, get to know	**lucir**	shine
reconocer	recognize	**conducir**	drive, conduct, lead
aparecer	appear	**producir**	produce
desaparecer	disappear	**reproducir**	reproduce
ofrecer	offer	**traducir**	translate
merecer	deserve		

(viii)   *-oy verbs*

In the following verbs, the first person singular form of the present indicative tense ends in **-oy.** The present subjunctive tense is not affected by this.

dar (give):   **doy, das, da, damos, dais, dan**
estar (be):   **estoy, estás, está, estamos, estáis, están**

Note: Ir (go) is irregular, but the present tense is quite predictable once established:

voy, vas, va, vamos, vais, van

(ix) *Pretérito grave*

A significant group of verbs have what is known as a **pretérito grave**. This refers to the fact that the first and third person singular preterite endings are not stressed and bear no accent. In addition, their set of preterite endings is a combination of the normal ones for **-ar** verbs (first and third person singular forms, but without accents) and **-er/-ir** verbs (all the rest).

tener (have):   **tuve, tuviste, tuvo, tuvimos, tuvisteis, tuvieron**

The following verbs also have a **pretérito grave**:

andar	→	anduve	poner	→	puse
caber	→	cupe	querer	→	quise
estar	→	estuve	saber	→	supe
haber	→	hube	tener	→	tuve
hacer	→	hice	venir	→	vine
poder	→	pude			

Note: Watch out for the following:

• The third person singular form of **hacer** is **hizo** in the preterite tense.
• When the stem of a **pretérito grave** ends in **-j-,** the third person plural ending is **-eron**.

decir	**dije**	**dijeron**
traer	**traje**	**trajeron**
conducir	**conduje**	**condujeron**

Compounds of the above verbs follow the same pattern [►10c]. Therefore, **componer** follows **poner, mantener** follows **tener**. Also, all verbs ending in **-ducir** follow the same pattern as **conducir**.

10c   Compound Verbs

A compound verb is a verb with a prefix attached to it. It is conjugated in the same way as the original verb ('base verb'), but the meaning is usually different, according to the prefix. Some base verbs can take many more prefixes than others can and thus give rise to a whole list of verbs with different meanings. Some common prefixes are **con-, contra-, des-, dis-, inter-, mal-, pre-, pro-, re-,** and so forth.

(i)   Compound verb formation with some of these prefixes follows.

• Prefix **contra-** (against) + base verb

hacer (do, make)	→	**contrahacer** (counterfeit, copy)

• Prefix **des-** (often corresponding to English 'un-' or 'de') + base verb

atar (tie)	→	**desatar** (untie)
congelar (freeze)	→	**descongelar** (unfreeze, deice)
cubrir (cover)	‣	**descubrir** (discover, uncover)
hacer (do)	→	**deshacer** (undo)

• Prefix **mal-** (meaning 'bad,' 'badly,' or 'evil') + base verb

gastar (spend)	→	**malgastar** (squander, waste)
decir (say)	→	**maldecir** (curse)

Note: The past participle of **maldecir** is **maldito.**

• Prefix **re-** (like English 're-,' but not used to the same extent to indicate repetition; often used to intensify) + base verb

hacer (do, make)	→	**rehacer** (remake)
vender (sell)	→	**revender** (resell)
llenar (fill)	→	**rellenar** (fill up, fill out)
mojar (wet)	→	**remojar** (soak, drench)
quemar (burn)	→	**requemar** (scorch, parch)

• Prefix **sobre-** (on, over) + base verb

venir (come)	→	**sobrevenir** (happen unexpectedly)

(ii)   **Poner** (put), **tener** (have), and **venir** (come) are among the verbs that can take many different prefixes.

• **Poner** has compounds that often correspond to English verbs ending in '-pose.'

componer	compose, mend
descomponerse	decompose, rot; break down (machine)
deponer	depose, lay down (arms, etc.)
imponer	impose
interponer	interpose
posponer	put behind, postpone

proponer	propose, suggest
reponer	replace, put back; reply
suponer	suppose
presuponer	presuppose

• **Tener** has compounds that correspond to English verbs ending in 'tain.'

contener	contain
detener	detain, stop
entretener	entertain, hold up, detain
mantener	maintain
retener	retain
sostener	sustain

• **Venir** has a number of compounds.

convenir	agree, suit
intervenir	intervene
provenir	come forth
sobrevenir	happen, occur (unexpectedly)

(iii)   Finally, you can detect the many different prefixes in words that passed into Spanish as compound words directly from Latin. In the words that follow, Latin **ducĕre** (lead) combined with the different Latin prefixes to give us:

conducir	conduct, lead, drive
deducir	deduce
inducir	induce, induct
introducir	introduce, insert
producir	produce
reducir	reduce
reproducir	reproduce
seducir	seduce
traducir	translate

Similarly, you can see how Spanish **satisfacer** (satisfy) is a direct descendant of Latin **satisfacer,** a word made up of **satis** (enough) + **facĕre** (do, make). **Satisfacer** is conjugated like **hacer.**

11 Reflexive Verbs

11a Reflexive Verbs in General

See section 2f for a general explanation of reflexive verbs. In addition to the verbs that are reflexive in English, Spanish treats many other verbs as reflexive. Many verbs can be used both as reflexive and as ordinary transitive verbs.

11b Reflexive Pronouns

The full set of reflexive pronouns accompanying these verbs can be seen in this example of the present indicative tense of the reflexive verb **lavarse** (wash oneself):

me lavo	I wash myself
te lavas	you wash yourself (informal)
se lava	he/she washes him-/herself,
	you wash yourself (formal)
nos lavamos	we wash ourselves
os laváis	you wash yourselves (informal)
se lavan	they wash themselves,
	you wash yourselves (formal)

11c Position of Reflexive Pronouns

Reflexive pronouns follow the same rules as other pronouns.

(A) They precede the verb:
• in all tenses of the indicative and the subjunctive;
• in all negative imperatives.

(B) They are joined to the end of the verb:
• in the gerund (optional);
• in all positive imperatives.

(C) With the infinitive, they can either precede the verb or be joined to the end of it.

Note: The stress pattern may require the use of a written accent to show that the stress stays the same.

¿Te lavas tú mismo, Paquito?	*Do you wash* all by *yourself*, Paquito?
No *te peines* así.	Don't *comb* your hair like that.
Estoy lavándome ahora mismo.	*I'm washing* right now.
¡Levántense inmediatamente!	*Get up* immediately!
Acuéstate a las diez.	Go to bed at ten.
Vamos a *bañarnos* en seguida.	
Nos vamos a *bañar* en seguida.	We are going *to take a bath* right now.

11d   Use of the Reflexive

Note that the reflexive form is often used in Spanish where one would use a possessive adjective in English.

Se lavaron las manos.	*They washed their* hands.
Mi novia *se pondrá el* vestido azul.	My girlfriend *will put on her* blue dress.

Note also the colloquial use of a reflexive form where normally the transitive form would be used, in order to intensify a statement or request.

Me comí todas las manzanas.	*I ate up* all the apples.

Note: The reflexive is often used to avoid a true passive [➤9b].

B

MODEL VERBS

Index of Model Verbs

Irregular verbs: *Number*

abrir	open; open up	25
adquirir	acquire; get; purchase	26
andar	walk; go around	27
bendecir	bless	28
caber	fit	29
caer(se)	fall, drop	30
conducir	drive; lead; conduct	31
conocer	know; get to know; meet	32
dar	give	33
decir	say; tell	34
erguir(se)	raise; lift; straighten up	35
errar	stray; wander; err	36
escribir	write	37
estar	be	38
freír	fry	39
haber	have (auxiliary)	40
hacer	do; make	41
ir	go	42
lucir(se)	shine; excel; show off	43
oír	hear; listen; pay attention	44
oler	smell; sniff	45
poder	be able to; can; may	46
poner	place; put; switch on	47
querer	want; wish; love	48
reír(se)	laugh	49
romper(se)	break	50
saber	know; know how to; learn	51
salir	get/go/come out; exit; leave	52
ser	be	53
tener	have; hold	54
traer	bring; fetch	55
valer	be worth; cost	56
venir	come	57
ver	see; watch	58

1 amar   love

Regular **-ar** verb

GERUND	*PAST PARTICIPLE*
amando	amado

ACTIVE VOICE

PRESENT INDICATIVE	*PRESENT PERFECT*
amo	he amado
amas	has amado
ama	ha amado
amamos	hemos amado
amáis	habéis amado
aman	han amado

PRESENT PROGRESSIVE	*IMPERFECT PROGRESSIVE*
estoy amando	estaba amando
estás amando	estabas amando
está amando	estaba amando
estamos amando	estábamos amando
estáis amando	estabais amando
están amando	estaban amando

IMPERFECT INDICATIVE	*PRETERITE*
amaba	amé
amabas	amaste
amaba	amó
amábamos	amamos
amabais	amasteis
amaban	amaron

PLUPERFECT	*PAST ANTERIOR*
había amado	hube amado
habías amado	hubiste amado
había amado	hubo amado
habíamos amado	hubimos amado
habíais amado	hubisteis amado
habían amado	hubieron amado

Note: See The Verb System in Spanish for explanations of the tenses. The important thing to note here is that all forms have the basic part, or stem, **am-**, which contains the meaning of the verb. Many tenses are simple tenses, in which endings are added to this stem to form just one word; other tenses are compound tenses, in which an auxiliary verb (helping verb) is used, in the appropriate tense and form, in

IMPERATIVE

(tú) ama	(vosotros) amad
(usted) ame	(ustedes) amen

FUTURE	*FUTURE PERFECT*
amaré	habré amado
amarás	habrás amado
amará	habrá amado
amaremos	habremos amado
amaréis	habréis amado
amarán	habrán amado

CONDITIONAL	*CONDITIONAL PERFECT*
amaría	habría/hubiera amado
amarías	habrías/hubieras amado
amaria	habría/hubiera amado
amaríamos	habríamos/hubiéramos amado
amaríais	habríais/hubierais amado
amarían	habrían/hubieran amado

PRESENT SUBJUNCTIVE	*PERFECT SUBJUNCTIVE*
ame	haya amado
ames	hayas amado
ame	haya amado
amemos	hayamos amado
améis	hayáis amado
amen	hayan amado

IMPERFECT SUBJUNCTIVE	*PLUPERFECT SUBJUNCTIVE*
amara/amase	hubiera/hubiese amado
amaras/amases	hubieras/hubieses amado
amara/amase	hubiera/hubiese amado
amáramos/amásemos	hubiéramos/hubiésemos amado
amarais/amaseis	hubierais/hubieseis amado
amaran/amasen	hubieran/hubiesen amado

front of the appropriate gerund or participle of the verb that contains the meaning. Remember that, in Spanish, the subject pronoun (**yo** = I, **tú** = you, etc.) is not normally needed because the verb endings are clear and distinct enough in both spoken and written forms; they are only needed for emphasis, contrast, or to avoid ambiguity.

1 amar   love

PASSIVE VOICE

For notes on other ways of expressing the passive, see The Verb System in Spanish.

PRESENT INDICATIVE

soy amado/a
eres amado/a
es amado/a
somos amados/as
sois amados/as
son amados/as

PRESENT PERFECT

he sido amado/a
has sido amado/a
ha sido amado/a
hemos sido amados/as
habéis sido amados/as
han sido amados/as

PRESENT PROGRESSIVE

estoy siendo amado/a
estás siendo amado/a
está siendo amado/a
estamos siendo amados/as
estáis siendo amados/as
están siendo amados/as

IMPERFECT PROGRESSIVE

estaba siendo amado/a
estabas siendo amado/a
estaba siendo amado/a
estábamos siendo amados/as
estabais siendo amados/as
estaban siendo amados/as

IMPERFECT INDICATIVE

era amado/a
eras amado/a
era amado/a
éramos amados/as
erais amados/as
eran amados/as

PRETERITE

fui amado/a
fuiste amado/a
fue amado/a
fuimos amados/as
fuisteis amados/as
fueron amados/as

PLUPERFECT

había sido amado/a
habías sido amado/a
había sido amado/a
habíamos sido amados/as
habíais sido amados/as
habían sido amados/as

PAST ANTERIOR

hube sido amado/a
hubiste sido amado/a
hubo sido amado/a
hubimos sido amados/as
hubisteis sido amados/as
hubieron sido amados/as

Jorge y Pedro *aman* a María, pero *ella* no *ama* a ninguno de los dos.

George and Peter *love* Mary, but she doesn't *love* either of them.

Si tus hermanos no te *amasen*, serías muy infeliz.

If your brothers and sisters *did*n't *love* you, you would be very unhappy.

FUTURE

seré amado/a
serás amado/a
será amado/a
seremos amados/as
seréis amados/as
serán amados/as

FUTURE PERFECT

habré sido amado/a
habrás sido amado/a
habrá sido amado/a
habremos sido amados/as
habréis sido amados/as
habrán sido amados/as

CONDITIONAL

sería amado/a
serías amado/a
sería amado/a
seríamos amados/as
seríais amados/as
serían amados/as

CONDITIONAL PERFECT

habría/hubiera sido amado/a
habrías/hubieras sido amado/a
habría/hubiera sido amado/a
habríamos/hubiéramos sido amados/as
habríais/hubierais sido amados/as
habrían/hubieran sido amados/as

PRESENT SUBJUNCTIVE

sea amado/a
seas amado/a
sea amado/a
seamos amados/as
seáis amados/as
sean amados/as

PERFECT SUBJUNCTIVE

haya amado/a
hayas amado/a
haya amado/a
hayamos amados/as
hayáis amados/as
hayan amados/as

IMPERFECT SUBJUNCTIVE

fuera/fuese amado/a
fueras/fueses amado/a
fuera/fuese amado/a
fuéramos/fuésemos amados/as

fuerais/fueseis amados/as
fueran/fuesen amados/as

PLUPERFECT SUBJUNCTIVE

hubiera/hubiese sido amado/a
hubieras/hubieses sido amado/a
hubiera/hubiese sido amado/a
hubiéramos/hubiésemos sido amados/as
hubierais/hubieseis sido amados/as
hubieran/hubiesen sido amados/as

Mi maestra *amaba* los animales. My teacher *loved* animals.

Ayer la *amabas*; aunque hoy ya no la *amas*, tal vez mañana la *amarás* otra vez. Yesterday *you loved* her; even though today *you* don't *love* her anymore, perhaps tomorrow *you will love* her again.

***Ellos se amaron* demasiado.** *They loved each other* too much.

Regular -ar verb

GERUND	PAST PARTICIPLE
comprando	comprado

PRESENT INDICATIVE	PRESENT PERFECT
compro	he comprado
compras	has comprado
compra	ha comprado
compramos ·	hemos comprado
compráis	habéis comprado
compran	han comprado

PRESENT PROGRESSIVE	IMPERFECT PROGRESSIVE
estoy comprando	estaba comprando

IMPERFECT INDICATIVE	PRETERITE
compraba	compré
comprabas	compraste
compraba	compró
comprábamos	compramos
comprabais	comprasteis
compraban	compraron

Note: The number of verbs that follow the regular -ar verb conjugation is very large, so the verbs given below are only a small selection of the most useful verbs of this group. In the Verb Index you can find the main meanings of each verb, and one or two can also be found in the reflexive form, sometimes with different meanings, e.g., **llamarse** 'to be called.' Other verbs apparently in this group may actually be major irregular verbs, have minor spelling irregularities, or be stem-changing verbs. For these verbs you should consult the relevant section of this book. Note that some of the forms of the -**ar** conjugation are quite similar to those of the -**er** and -**ir** verbs, and that the following are the same:
- the first person singular (**yo**) ending in the present indicative tense;
- the auxiliary verbs for the compound tenses; and
- the formation and endings of the future tense.

Similar verbs

Only very few of the most commonly used –**ar** verbs are listed here.

ayudar	help	**dejar**	leave, let
bajar	go down	**entrar**	enter

IMPERATIVE

(tú) compra   (vosotros) comprad
(usted) compre   (ustedes) compren

PLUPERFECT   *PAST ANTERIOR*
había comprado   hube comprado

FUTURE   *FUTURE PERFECT*
compraré   habré comprado

CONDITIONAL   *CONDITIONAL PERFECT*
compraría   habría/hubiera comprado

PRESENT SUBJUNCTIVE   *PERFECT SUBJUNCTIVE*
compre   haya comprado

IMPERFECT SUBJUNCTIVE   *PLUPERFECT SUBJUNCTIVE*
comprara/comprase   hubiera/hubiese comprado

---

ganar	earn	**mirar**	look, see, watch
hablar	talk, speak	**pasar**	pass, spend
lavar	wash	**quedarse**	stay
levantarse	get up	**tomar**	take
llamar	call	**trabajar**	work
llevar	carry, wear		

¡Qué ambicioso!

—¿A qué hora *te levantas?*

—A las siete.

—¿Por qué tan temprano?

—Quiero *trabajar* mucho.

—¿Por qué?

—Para *ganar* mucho dinero. Un día voy a *comprarme* una casa muy grande, *pasaré* mis vacaciones en Europa, y... ¡entonces me voy a *quedar* en la cama hasta mediodía! ¡Es por eso que ahora *trabajo* tanto!

What an ambitious guy!

"At what time *do you get up*?"

"At seven."

"Why so early?"

"I want to *work* a lot."

"Why?"

"To *earn* lots of money. One day I am going to *buy* a very big house, *I* will *spend* my vacations in Europe and,... then *I* will *stay* in bed until noon! That's why *I'm working* so hard now!"

3 comer   eat

Regular **-er** verb

GERUND	**PAST PARTICIPLE**
comiendo	comido

PRESENT INDICATIVE	**PRESENT PERFECT**
como	he comido
comes	has comido
come	ha comido
comemos	hemos comido
coméis	habéis comido
comen	han comido

PRESENT PROGRESSIVE	**IMPERFECT PROGRESSIVE**
estoy comiendo	estaba comiendo

IMPERFECT INDICATIVE	**PRETERITE**
comía	comí
comías	comiste
comía	comió
comíamos	comimos
comíais	comisteis
comían	comieron

Similar verbs

Only some of the most commonly used **-er** verbs are listed here.

aprender	learn	**sorprender**	surprise; catch out
beber	drink	**suceder**	succeed, happen
correr	run	**suspender**	give a failing grade
coser	sew	**temer**	fear
deber	owe, must	**toser**	cough
prometer	promise	**vender**	sell

Note: Although the **-er** group of verbs is a large one, many are irregular or are subject to spelling changes. These verbs appear in the appropriate sections of this book; those appearing above are entirely regular. Many of these verbs can be used in both reflexive and non-relexive form; the list gives the most commonly used form. Note that some of the forms of the **-er** conjugation are very similar to those of the **-ar** verbs, and that the following are the same as for both **-ar** and **-ir** verbs:
- the first person singular (**yo**) ending in the present indicative tense;
- the auxiliary verbs for the compound tenses; and
- the formation and endings of the future tense.

IMPERATIVE
(tú) come
(usted) coma

(vosotros) comed
(ustedes) coman

PLUPERFECT
había comido

PAST ANTERIOR
hube comido

FUTURE
comeré

FUTURE PERFECT
habré comido

CONDITIONAL
comería

CONDITIONAL PERFECT
habría/hubiera comido

PRESENT SUBJUNCTIVE
coma

PERFECT SUBJUNCTIVE
haya comido

IMPERFECT SUBJUNCTIVE
comprara/comprase

PLUPERFECT SUBJUNCTIVE
hubiera/hubiese comido

The following forms are the same as for **-ir** verbs:
- four out of six of the present indicative forms;
- the gerund (or present participle) and the past participle;
- the preterite and the imperfect indicative tenses

¡Qué alumno más malo!	**What an awful pupil!**
—¿Qué le *sucede* a Sánchez? ¡No *aprende* nada!	"What's happening to Sánchez? He learns nothing!"
—Es que pasa todo su tiempo libre *vendiendo* periódicos en la calle. Quiere comprar un automóvil, por eso *debe* ganar dinero....	"He's spending all his free time selling newspapers on the street. He wants to buy a car, so he has to earn money. . . ."
—Ayer, Sánchez *prometió* que, de aquí en adelante, *aprenderá* todo muy bien.	"Yesterday, Sánchez promised that, from now on, he will learn everything well."
—Espero que sí. Si no, *temo* que el profesor lo va a *suspender*.	"I hope so. If not, I fear the teacher is going to give him, a failing grade."

4 vivir   live

Regular **-ir** verb

GERUND	*PAST PARTICIPLE*
viviendo	vivido

PRESENT INDICATIVE	*PRESENT PERFECT*
vivo	he vivido
vives	has vivido
vive	ha vivido
vivimos	hemos vivido
vivís	habéis vivido
viven	han vivido

PRESENT PROGRESSIVE	*IMPERFECT PROGRESSIVE*
estoy viviendo	estaba viviendo

IMPERFECT INDICATIVE	*PRETERITE*
vivía	viví
vivías	viviste
vivía	vivió
vivíamos	vivimos
vivíais	vivisteis
vivían	vivieron

Similar verbs

Only some of the most commonly used **-ir** verbs are listed here.

aburrir	bore	**dividir**	divide
admitir	accept	**partir**	depart, split
asistir	attend, assist	**persuadir**	persuade
consistir	consist	**sobrevivir**	survive
convivir	live together, coexist	**subir**	go up, raise
decidir	decide	**sufrir**	suffer
discutir	discuss	**unir**	unite
distinguir	distinguish		

Note: The **-ir** group of verbs is very large, but many are irregular or are subject to spelling changes. These verbs appear in the appropriate sections of this book; those listed above are entirely regular. Many of the listed verbs can be used in both reflexive and nonreflexive forms; the most commonly used forms are given in the above list. Note that some of the forms of the **-ir** conjugation are similar to or the same as those of the **-ar** and **-er** verbs. The following are the same as for both **-ar** and **-er** verbs:
- the first person singular (**yo**) ending in the present indicative tense;
- the auxiliary verbs for the compound tenses; and
- the formation and endings of the future tense.

IMPERATIVE

(tú) vive	(vosotros) vivid
(usted) viva	(ustedes) vivan

PLUPERFECT había vivido	**PAST ANTERIOR** hube vivido
FUTURE viviré	**FUTURE PERFECT** habré vivido
CONDITIONAL viviría	**CONDITIONAL PERFECT** habría/hubiera vivido
PRESENT SUBJUNCTIVE viva	**PERFECT SUBJUNCTIVE** haya vivido
IMPERFECT SUBJUNCTIVE viviera/viviese	**PLUPERFECT SUBJUNCTIVE** hubiera/hubiese vivido

The following forms are the same as for **-er** verbs:

- four out of six of the present indicative forms;
- the gerund (or present participle) and the past participle;
- the preterite and the imperfect indicative tenses.

¡Qué muchacho más dificil!	**What a difficult guy!**
Tomás es un joven que *se aburre* muy fácilmente. Su único interés real *consiste* en leer y escribir, y en hablar sobre lo que lee y escribe. Sus amigos *sufren* mucho por esto, porque nunca pueden *persuadirlo* para que salga con ellos. Además, él siempre quiere que la casa esté tranquila. Es muy difícil *vivir* con un muchacho como Tomás, pero sus amigos lo quieren. Por eso *han decidido* que permanecerán juntos y no se separarán.	Thomas is a young man who *gets bored* very easily. His only real interest *consists* of reading and writing and of talking about what he reads and writes. His friends *suffer* a lot out of this, because they can never *persuade him* to go out with them. Besides, he always wants the house to be quiet. It's hard *to live* with a guy like Thomas, but his friends love him. So *they have decided* that they will stay together and will not seperate.

53

-ar verbs: **c** → **qu**

GERUND	PAST PARTICIPLE
sacando	sacado

PRESENT INDICATIVE	PRESENT PERFECT
saco	he sacado

PRESENT PROGRESSIVE	IMPERFECT PROGRESSIVE
estoy sacando	estaba sacando

IMPERFECT INDICATIVE	PRETERITE
sacaba	saqué
	sacaste
	sacó
	sacamos
	sacasteis
	sacaron

PLUPERFECT	PAST ANTERIOR
había sacado	hube sacado

Similar verbs

aparcar	park	**buscar**	look for, search
aplicar	apply	**confiscar**	confiscate
arrancar	start up	**criticar**	criticize
atacar	attack	**tocar**	touch, play (instrument)
atracar	assault, mug; moor, tie up		

Note: The **-c-** changes to **-qu-** before verb endings beginning with an **-e-**, in order to preserve the sound. In all other respects these verbs are regular. There are verbs other than the ones above that have the **c** → **qu** change, but they are not listed here because they are stem-changing verbs.

IMPERATIVE

(tú) saca	(vosotros) sacad
(usted) saque	(ustedes) saquen

FUTURE
sacaré

FUTURE PERFECT
habré sacado

CONDITIONAL
sacaría

CONDITIONAL PERFECT
habría / hubiera sacado

PRESENT SUBJUNCTIVE
saque
saques
saque
saquemos
saquéis
saquen

PERFECT SUBJUNCTIVE
haya sacado

IMPERFECT SUBJUNCTIVE
sacara / sacase

PLUPERFECT SUBJUNCTIVE
hubiera / hubiese sacado

El atraco

El sábado pasado, fui víctima de un atraco. Al llegar al centro ciudad, *busqué* un sitio para dejar el coche. Por fin *aparqué* en una calle oscura. Cuando bajé del coche, alguien me *tocó* en la espalda con una navaja. El ladrón me dijo: "*Saque* el monedero". En lugar del monedero, *saqué* mi alarma personal. Con el ruido, *el hombre que me atacó* se fue corriendo.

The mugging

Last Saturday I was the victim of a mugging. When I got downtown, *I looked for* a place to park the car. Finally, *I parked* on a dark street. As I got out of the car, someone *touched* me in the back with a knife. The mugger said, "*Take out* your wallet." Instead of the wallet, *I took out* my personal alarm. With the noise, *the attacker* ran off.

6 cazar   hunt, chase

-ar verbs: **z** → **c**

GERUND	*PAST PARTICIPLE*
cazando	cazado

PRESENT INDICATIVE	*PRESENT PERFECT*
cazo	he cazado

PRESENT PROGRESSIVE	*IMPERFECT PROGRESSIVE*
estoy cazando	estaba cazando

IMPERFECT INDICATIVE	*PRETERITE*
cazaba	cacé
	cazaste
	cazó
	cazamos
	cazasteis
	cazaron

PLUPERFECT	*PAST ANTERIOR*
había cazado	hube cazado

Similar verbs

abrazar	hug, embrace	**lanzar**	launch, throw
avergonzarse	be ashamed	**rezar**	pray

Note: The **-z-** changes to **-c-** before verb endings beginning with an **-e-**. In all other respects these verbs are regular. There are quite a few verbs other than the ones listed above that have the **z** → **c** change, but they are not listed here because they are stem-changing verbs.

IMPERATIVE

(tú) caza   (vosotros) cazad
(usted) cace   (ustedes) cacen

FUTURE
cazaré

FUTURE PERFECT
habré cazado

CONDITIONAL
cazaría

CONDITIONAL PERFECT
habría/hubiera cazado

PRESENT SUBJUNCTIVE
cace
caces
cace
cacemos
cacéis
cacen

PERFECT SUBJUNCTIVE
haya cazado

IMPERFECT SUBJUNCTIVE
cazara/cazase

PLUPERFECT SUBJUNCTIVE
hubiera/hubiese cazado

Me avergoncé de no pasar el examen.

I was ashamed of falling the exam.

Mi madre estaba rezando en la Iglesia cuando lanzaron una bomba en un edificio cercano.

My mother *was praying* in church when *they threw* a bomb into a nearby building.

Él nos abrazó y partió.

He embraced us and left.

No te avergüences de abrazar a alguien en público.

Don't be ashamed of hugging someone in public.

7 pagar   pay

-ar verbs: **g** → **gu**

GERUND	PAST PARTICIPLE
pagando	pagado

PRESENT INDICATIVE	PRESENT PERFECT
pago	he pagado

PRESENT PROGRESSIVE	IMPERFECT PROGRESSIVE
estoy pagando	estaba pagando

IMPERFECT INDICATIVE	PRETERITE
pagaba	pagué
	pagaste
	pagó
	pagamos
	pagasteis
	pagaron

PLUPERFECT	PAST ANTERIOR
había pagado	hube pagado

Similar verbs

apagar	put out, switch off, turn off	**obligar**	oblige; force
llegar	arrive; reach		

Note: The **-g-** changes to **-gu-** before verb endings beginning with **-e-,** in order to preserve the sound. In all other respects these verbs are regular. There are quite a few verbs other than the ones listed above that have the **g** → **gu** change, but are not listed here because they are stem-changing verbs.

IMPERATIVE
(tú) paga
(usted) pague

(vosotros) pagad
(ustedes) paguen

FUTURE	**FUTURE PERFECT**
pagaré	habré pagado

CONDITIONAL
pagaría

CONDITIONAL PERFECT
habría/hubiera pagado

PRESENT SUBJUNCTIVE
pague
pagues
pague
paguemos
paguéis
paguen

PERFECT SUBJUNCTIVE
haya pagado

IMPERFECT SUBJUNCTIVE
pagara/pagase

PLUPERFECT SUBJUNCTIVE
hubiera/hubiese pagado

Espero que me *pagues* pronto.

I hope *you will pay* me soon.

***Paguen* la cuenta, señores; no me *obliguen* a llamar a la policía.**

Pay the bill, gentlemen; *do* not *force* me to call the police.

Si los bomberos *hubieran llegado* a tiempo, *habrían apagado* el incendio.

If the firemen *had arrived* on time, *they would have put out* the fire.

8 averiguar   verify; find out; look up

-ar verbs: **gu** → **gü**

GERUND	PAST PARTICIPLE
averiguando	averiguado

PRESENT INDICATIVE	PRESENT PERFECT
averiguo	he averiguado

PRESENT PROGRESSIVE	IMPERFECT PROGRESSIVE
estoy averiguando	estaba averiguando

IMPERFECT INDICATIVE	PRETERITE
averiguaba	averigüé
	averiguaste
	averiguó
	averiguamos
	averiguasteis
	averiguaron

PLUPERFECT	PAST ANTERIOR
había averiguado	hube averiguado

Similar verbs

amortiguar   deaden, muffle   **apaciguar**   pacify, appease

Note: The **-gu-** changes to **-gü-** before verb endings beginning with an **-e-**, in order to preserve the sound. In all other respects these verbs are regular.

IMPERATIVE
(tú) averigua
(usted) averigüe

(vosotros) averiguad
(ustedes) averigüen

FUTURE
averiguaré

FUTURE PERFECT
habré averiguado

CONDITIONAL
averiguaría

CONDITIONAL PERFECT
habría/hubiera averiguado

PRESENT SUBJUNCTIVE
averigüe
averigües
averigüe
averigüemos
averigüéis
averigüen

PERFECT SUBJUNCTIVE
haya averiguado

IMPERFECT SUBJUNCTIVE
averiguara/averiguase

PLUPERFECT SUBJUNCTIVE
hubiera/hubiese averiguado

Ayer *averigüé* dónde se obtiene la licencia de conducir.

Yesterday *I found out* where you can get a driver's license.

Las paredes *amortiguaban* los ruidos.

The walls *muffled* the noises.

Apacigüe su sed con agua, no con vino.

Quench your thirst with water, not with wine.

9 vencer   win; defeat

-er and **-ir** verbs: **c** → **z**

GERUND	PAST PARTICIPLE
venciendo	vencido

PRESENT INDICATIVE	PRESENT PERFECT
venzo	he vencido
vences	
vence	
vencemos	
vencéis	
vencen	

PRESENT PROGRESSIVE	IMPERFECT PROGRESSIVE
estoy venciendo	estaba venciendo

IMPERFECT INDICATIVE	PRETERITE
vencía	vencí

PLUPERFECT	PAST ANTERIOR
había vencido	hube vencido

Similar verbs

convencer	convince	**esparcir**	scatter, spread
ejercer	exercise, exert	**mecer**	rock, swing

Note: The **-c-** changes to **-z-** before verb endings beginning with an **-a-** or an **-o-**, in order to preserve the sound. In all other respects these verbs are regular. There are verbs other than the ones listed above that have the **c** → **z** change, but they are not listed here because they are stem-changing verbs.

IMPERATIVE
(tú) vence	(vosotros) venced
(usted) venza	(ustedes) venzan

FUTURE
venceré

FUTURE PERFECT
habré vencido

CONDITIONAL
vencería

CONDITIONAL PERFECT
habría/hubiera vencido

PRESENT SUBJUNCTIVE
venza
venzas
venza
venzamos
venzáis
venzan

PERFECT SUBJUNCTIVE
haya vencido

IMPERFECT SUBJUNCTIVE
venciera/venciese

PLUPERFECT SUBJUNCTIVE
hubiera/hubiese vencido

Yo no *ejerzo* ninguna influencia sobre mi hermano.	*I exert* no influence on my brother.
Esparza las semillas sobre la tierra.	*Scatter* the seeds on the ground.
Finalmente la *convencí* para que se quedara en casa con su madre.	*I finally convinced* her to stay home with her mother.
No me *convences* ...	*You* don't *convince* me. . . .
Meza la cuna de su bebé con cuidado.	*Rock* your baby's cradle carefully.

10 distinguir   distinguish; make out

-er and **-ir** verbs: **gu** → **g**

GERUND	*PAST PARTICIPLE*
distinguiendo	distinguido

PRESENT INDICATIVE	*PRESENT PERFECT*
distingo	he distinguido
distingues	
distingue	
distinguimos	
distinguís	
distinguen	

PRESENT PROGRESSIVE	*IMPERFECT PROGRESSIVE*
estoy distinguiendo	estaba distinguiendo

IMPERFECT INDICATIVE	*PRETERITE*
distinguía	distinguí

PLUPERFECT	*PAST ANTERIOR*
había distinguido	hube distinguido

Similar verb

extinguir   extinguish, put out

Note: The **-gu-** changes to **-g-** before verb endings beginning with an **-o-** or
         an **-a-**. In all other respects these verbs are regular. There are verbs
         other than **distinguir** and **extinguir** that have the **g** → **gu** change, but
         they are not listed here because they are stem-changing verbs.

IMPERATIVE
(tú) distingue
(usted) distinga

(vosotros) distinguid
(ustedes) distingan

FUTURE
distinguiré

FUTURE PERFECT
habré distinguido

CONDITIONAL
distinguiría

CONDITIONAL PERFECT
habría/hubiera distinguido

PRESENT SUBJUNCTIVE
distinga
distingas
distinga
distingamos
distingáis
distingan

PERFECT SUBJUNCTIVE
haya distinguido

IMPERFECT SUBJUNCTIVE
distinguiera/distinguiese

PLUPERFECT SUBJUNCTIVE
hubiera/hubiese distinguido

Hace falta que *distingas* entre los dos.

You need to *distinguish* between the two of them.

Los bomberos *extinguieron* el fuego.

The firefighters *extinguished* the fire.

Sin mis lentes, no *distingo* bien las cosas.

Without my glasses, I don't *make out* things well.

11 coger   take, catch

-er and **-ir** verbs: **g** → **j**

GERUND	PAST PARTICIPLE
cogiendo	cogido

PRESENT INDICATIVE	PRESENT PERFECT
cojo	he cogido
coges	
coge	
cogemos	
cogéis	
cogen	

PRESENT PROGRESSIVE	IMPERFECT PROGRESSIVE
estoy cogiendo	estaba cogiendo

IMPERFECT INDICATIVE	PRETERITE
cogía	cogí

PLUPERFECT	PAST ANTERIOR
había cogido	hube cogido

Similar verbs

acoger	welcome	**proteger**	protect
escoger	choose	**restringir**	restrict
fingir	feign, pretend		

Note: The **-g-** changes to **-j-** before verb endings beginning with an **-a-** or an **-o-** in order to preserve the sound. In all other respects these verbs are regular. There are verbs other than the ones listed above that have the **g** → **j** change, but they are not listed here because they are stem-changing verbs.

IMPERATIVE

(tú) coge	(vosotros) coged
(usted) coja	(ustedes) cojan

FUTURE	**FUTURE PERFECT**
cogeré	habré cogido

CONDITIONAL	**CONDITIONAL PERFECT**
cogería	habría/hubiera cogido

PRESENT SUBJUNCTIVE	**PERFECT SUBJUNCTIVE**
coja	haya cogido
cojas	
coja	
cojamos	
cojáis	
cojan	

IMPERFECT SUBJUNCTIVE	**PLUPERFECT SUBJUNCTIVE**
cogiera/cogiese	hubiera/hubiese cogido

¡*Cojan* todo lo que puedan!	*Take* everything you can!
Cuando voy al cine, siempre *escojo* una película extranjera.	When I go to the movies, *I* always *choose* a foreign film.
Nos *acogieron* en su hogar como si fueramos parte de su familia.	*They welcomed* us in their home as if we were part of their family.
Restringe tus gastos, y *protegerás* tu futuro.	*Restrict* your expenses, and you *will protect* your future.

-uir verbs: **i** → **y**

GERUND	PAST PARTICIPLE
huyendo	huido

PRESENT INDICATIVE	PRESENT PERFECT
huyo	he huido
huyes	
huye	
huimos	
huís	
huyen	

PRESENT PROGRESSIVE	IMPERFECT PROGRESSIVE
estoy huyendo	estaba huyendo

IMPERFECT INDICATIVE	PRETERITE
huía	huí
	huiste
	huyó
	huimos
	huisteis
	huyeron

Similar verbs

concluir	conclude	**disminuir**	diminish, lessen
construir	build, construct	**excluir**	exclude
destruir	destroy	**incluir**	include
distribuir	distribute	**influir**	influence

Note: The **-i-** is replaced by **-y-** to avoid having three vowels together. In all other respects these verbs are regular.

IMPERATIVE

(tú) huye	(vosotros) huid
(usted) huya	(ustedes) huyan

PLUPERFECT	**PAST ANTERIOR**
había huido	hube huido
FUTURE	**FUTURE PERFECT**
huiré	habré huido
CONDITIONAL	**CONDITIONAL PERFECT**
huiría	habría/hubiera huido
PRESENT SUBJUNCTIVE	**PERFECT SUBJUNCTIVE**
huya	haya huido
huyas	
huya	
huyamos	
huyáis	
huyan	
IMPERFECT SUBJUNCTIVE	**PLUPERFECT SUBJUNCTIVE**
huyera/huyese	hubiera/hubiese huido

¡Huye, que ya viene la policía!	*Run,* the police are coming!
Los moros construyeron esta casa.	The Moors *built* this house.
El juez concluyó que el reo era inocente.	The judge *concluded* that the prisoner was innocent.
Los impuestos están incluidos en el precio.	The taxes *are included* in the price.

13 leer   read

-eer verbs: take a **-y-** between vowels

GERUND	PAST PARTICIPLE
leyendo	leído

PRESENT INDICATIVE	PRESENT PERFECT
leo	he leído

PRESENT PROGRESSIVE	IMPERFECT PROGRESSIVE
estoy leyendo	estaba leyendo

IMPERFECT INDICATIVE	PRETERITE
leía	leí
	leíste
	leyó
	leímos
	leísteis
	leyeron

PLUPERFECT	PAST ANTERIOR
había leído	hube leído

Similar verbs

creer   believe   **poseer**   possess, own, have

Note: The **-i-** is replaced by **-y-** to avoid having three vowels together in certain forms (including the imperfect subjunctive); in others the **-i-** takes a written accent to keep the stress in the correct place. In all other respects these verbs are regular. Note that **caer** (fall) and **oír** (hear) have a similar spelling change, but are also irregular in other ways.

70

IMPERATIVE

(tú) lee   (vosotros) leed
(usted) lea   (ustedes) lean

FUTURE   *FUTURE PERFECT*

leeré   habré leído

CONDITIONAL   *CONDITIONAL PERFECT*

leería   habría/hubiera leído

PRESENT SUBJUNCTIVE   *PERFECT SUBJUNCTIVE*

lea   haya leído
leas
lea
leamos
leáis
lean

IMPERFECT SUBJUNCTIVE   *PLUPERFECT SUBJUNCTIVE*

leyera/leyese   hubiera/hubiese leído

¿*Leyeron* la noticias sobre la guerra?

Did you read the news about the war?

***Ellos* no *creían* lo que estaban *leyendo*.**

They didn't believe what they *were reading.*

Roberto *tenía* dos defectos: nunca *leía*, y no *creía* en nada.

Robert *had* two faults: *he* never *read*, and *he* didn't *believe* in anything.

14 enviar   send

GERUND	PAST PARTICIPLE
enviando	enviado

PRESENT INDICATIVE	PRESENT PERFECT
envío	he enviado
envías	
envía	
enviamos	
enviáis	
envían	

PRESENT PROGRESSIVE	IMPERFECT PROGRESSIVE
estoy enviando	estaba enviando

IMPERFECT INDICATIVE	PRETERITE
enviaba	envié

PLUPERFECT	PAST ANTERIOR
había enviado	hube enviado

Similar verbs

confiar	confide, entrust	fiarse	trust
criar	rear, bring up, raise	guiar	guide
desafiar	challenge, defy	liar	bind, tie
desviar	divert, detour	vaciar	empty

Note: These -iar verbs require an accent on the -i- when it is stressed in a
conjugation, as shown above. The endings are all regular. Note also
that some verbs require an accent on the -i- of the stem when it is
stressed aislar (isolate) and prohibir (prohibit).

IMPERATIVE
(tú) envía
(usted) envíe
(vosotros) enviad
(ustedes) envíen

FUTURE
enviaré

FUTURE PERFECT
habré enviado

PERFECT
enviaría

CONDITIONAL PERFECT
habría/hubiera enviado

PRESENT SUBJUNCTIVE
envíe
envíes
envíe
enviemos
enviéis
envíen

PERFECT SUBJUNCTIVE
haya enviado

IMPERFECT SUBJUNCTIVE
enviara/enviase

PLUPERFECT SUBJUNCTIVE
hubiera/hubiese enviado

Pepe *criaba* ovejas en Alcalá. — Pepe *used to raise* sheep in Alcalá.

Vacíen sus bolsillos. — *Empty* your pockets.

Mi amigo me *confió* un secreto. — My friend *told* me a secret.

Te *desafío* a una carrera. — *I challenge* you to a race.

73

verbs with stressed weak vowel: **u** → **ú**

GERUND	*PAST PARTICIPLE*
actuando	actuado

PRESENT INDICATIVE	*PRESENT PERFECT*
actúo	he actuado
actúas	
actúa	
actuamos	
actuáis	
actúan	

PRESENT PROGRESSIVE	*IMPERFECT PROGRESSIVE*
estoy actuando	estaba actuando

IMPERFECT INDICATIVE	*PRETERITE*
actuaba	actué

PLUPERFECT	*PAST ANTERIOR*
había actuado	hube actuado

Similar verbs

continuar	continue	**exceptuar**	except
devaluar	devalue	**insinuar**	insinuate, suggest
evaluar	evaluate	**perpetuar**	perpetuate

Note: The accent is needed on certain forms to keep the stress in the correct place. The endings are regular. The verb **reunir(se)** (join) needs an accent on the **-u-** when it is stressed.

IMPERATIVE
(tú) actúa   (vosotros) actuad
(usted) actúe   (ustedes) actúen

FUTURE   *FUTURE PERFECT*
actuaré   habré actuado

CONDITIONAL   *CONDITIONAL PERFECT*
actuaría   habría/hubiera actuado

PRESENT SUBJUNCTIVE   *PERFECT SUBJUNCTIVE*
actúe   haya actuado
actúes
actúe
actuemos
actueis
actúen

IMPERFECT SUBJUNCTIVE   *PLUPERFECT SUBJUNCTIVE*
actuara/actuase   hubiera/hubiese actuado

Pese a que se lo *insinúo* siempre, Ana *actúa* como si no entendiera.

Although *I* always *suggest* it to her, Anna *acts* as if she didn't understand.

Antes de que el gobierno *devalúe* la moneda, es necesario que los economistas *evalúen* los efectos.

Before the government *devalues* the currency, it is necessary that the economists *evaluate* the effects.

Continúa ensayando hasta que *actúes* bien.

Continue rehearsing until you *act* well.

16 zambullir(se) dive, plunge (into water); dip

verbs whose stems end in -ll-

GERUND	PAST PARTICIPLE
zambullendo	zambullido

PRESENT INDICATIVE	PRESENT PERFECT
zambullo	he zambullido

PRESENT PROGRESSIVE	IMPERFECT PROGRESSIVE
estoy zambullendo	estaba zambullendo

IMPERFECT INDICATIVE	PRETERITE
zambullía	zambullí
	zambulliste
	zambulló
	zambullimos
	zambullisteis
	zambulleron

PLUPERFECT	PAST ANTERIOR
había zambullido	hube zambullido

Similar verbs

engullir   gobble, gulp   **escabullirse**   slip away

Note: Due to the **-ll-**, the **-i-** disappears in certain forms, as shown above, when followed by another — stressed — vowel.

IMPERATIVE
(tú) zambulle
(usted) zambulla

(vosotros) zambullid
(ustedes) zambullan

FUTURE
zambulliré

FUTURE PERFECT
habré zambullido

CONDITIONAL
zambulliría

CONDITIONAL PERFECT
habría/hubiera zambullido

PRESENT SUBJUNCTIVE
zambulla

PERFECT SUBJUNCTIVE
haya zambullido

IMPERFECT SUBJUNCTIVE
zambullera/zambullese
zambulleras/zambulleses
zambullera/zambullese
zambulléramos/zambullésemos
zambullerais/zambulleseis
zambulleran/zambullesen

PLUPERFECT SUBJUNCTIVE
hubiera/hubiese zambullido

El ladrón *se escabulló* con las joyas.

The thief *slipped away* with the jewels.

Están zambulléndose en la piscina.

They're diving into the swimming pool.

¡No *engullas* la comida!

Don't *gobble* the food!

17 gruñir   grunt

verbs whose stems end in -ñ-

GERUND	PAST PARTICIPLE
gruñendo	gruñido

PRESENT INDICATIVE	PRESENT PERFECT
gruño	he gruñido

PRESENT PROGRESSIVE	IMPERFECT PROGRESSIVE
estoy gruñendo	estaba gruñendo

IMPERFECT INDICATIVE	PRETERITE
gruñía	gruñí
	gruñiste
	gruñó
	gruñimos
	gruñisteis
	gruñeron

PLUPERFECT	PAST ANTERIOR
había gruñido	hube gruñido

Similar verbs

ceñir	gird, surround, skirt	**tañer**	play, pluck (*instrument*)
reñir	scold, quarrel	**teñir**	dye

Note: Due to the -ñ-, the -i- disappears in certain forms, as shown above, when followed by another — stressed — vowel.

IMPERATIVE

(tú) gruñe	(vosotros) gruñid
(usted) gruña	(ustedes) gruñan

FUTURE	*FUTURE PERFECT*
gruñiré	habré gruñido

CONDITIONAL	*CONDITIONAL PERFECT*
gruñiría	habría/hubiera gruñido

PRESENT SUBJUNCTIVE	*PERFECT SUBJUNCTIVE*
gruña	haya gruñido

IMPERFECT SUBJUNCTIVE   *PLUPERFECT SUBJUNCTIVE*

gruñera/gruñese   hubiera/hubiese gruñido
gruneras/gruñeses
gruñera/gruñese
gruñéramos/gruñésemos
gruñerais/gruñeseis
gruñeran/gruñesen

La profesora *riñó* a las chicas.	The teacher *scolded* the girls.
Los músicos *tañeron* suavemente sus arpas.	The musicians *plucked* their harps softly.
Mi padre *gruñe* cada vez que se enoja.	My father *grunts* whenever he is upset.

forms with a **-g-**

GERUND	PAST PARTICIPLE
asiendo	asido

PRESENT INDICATIVE	PRESENT PERFECT
asgo	he asido
ases	
ase	
asimos	
asís	
asen	

PRESENT PROGRESSIVE	IMPERFECT PROGRESSIVE
estoy asiendo	estaba asiendo

IMPERFECT INDICATIVE	PRETERITE
asía	así

PLUPERFECT	PAST ANTERIOR
había asido	hube asido

Note: In practice, the forms containing a **-g-** should not be used. To avoid them, use a different verb.

IMPERATIVE

(tú) ase

(usted) asga

(vosotros) asid

(ustedes) asgan

FUTURE	*FUTURE PERFECT*
asiré	habré asido

CONDITIONAL	*CONDITIONAL PERFECT*
asiría	habría/hubiera asido

PRESENT SUBJUNCTIVE

asga

asgas

asga

asgamos

asgáis

asgan

PERFECT SUBJUNCTIVE

haya asido

IMPERFECT SUBJUNCTIVE

aslera/asiese

PLUPERFECT SUBJUNCTIVE

hubiera/hubiese asido

Me *así* a la barra para *evitar* caer.   *I grabbed* the bar to avoid falling.

¡*Ásgate* a esa rama!   *Grasp* that branch!

19 pensar   think

type 1 stem-changing verb **e** → **ie**

GERUND	PAST PARTICIPLE
pensando	pensado

PRESENT INDICATIVE	PRESENT PERFECT
pienso	he pensado
piensas	
piensa	
pensamos	
pensáis	
piensan	

PRESENT PROGRESSIVE	IMPERFECT PROGRESSIVE
estoy pensando	estaba pensando

IMPERFECT INDICATIVE	PRETERITE
pensaba	pensé
	pensaste
	pensó
	pensamos
	pensasteis
	pensaron

Similar verbs

Only a very small selection of **e** → **ie** stem-changing verbs is listed here.

cerrar	close	**encender**	light, switch on
comenzar	commence, start	**entender**	understand
empezar	begin	**sentarse**	sit down

Note: These verbs are type 1 stem-changing verbs. They are irregular only in the present indicative and present subjunctive tenses, and thus also in the imperative forms except for the **vosotros** form (**pensad**). What happens is that the **-e-** in the stem changes to **-ie-** in those forms in which the stress falls on the syllable containing the **-e-**. In the forms that have the stress on the ending, the **-e-** remains. Note that some are **-ar** verbs and some are **-er** verbs; the regular endings for each group should be used. Verbs ending in **-zar** and **-gar** are also spelling-change verbs: ➤ Model Verbs 6 and 7, respectively.

IMPERATIVE

(tú) piensa   (vosotros) pensad
(usted) piense   (ustedes) piensen

PLUPERFECT   **PAST ANTERIOR**
había pensado   hube pensado

FUTURE   **FUTURE PERFECT**
pensaré   habré pensado

CONDITIONAL   **CONDITIONAL PERFECT**
pensaría   habría/hubiera pensado

PRESENT SUBJUNCTIVE   **PERFECT SUBJUNCTIVE**
piense   haya pensado
pienses
piense
pensemos
penséis
piensen

IMPERFECT SUBJUNCTIVE   **PLUPERFECT SUBJUNCTIVE**
pensara/pensase   hubiera/hubiese pensado

Cuando hace frío   **When it is cold**

Si hace frío, lo mejor es que   If it is cold, the best thing to do is to
cierres **la ventana. Luego,**   *close* the window. Then, *light* a fire
enciende **el fuego en la chimenea,** in the fireplace and *start* calling
y *comienza* **a llamar a tus amigos.** your friends. Once they are all at
Una vez que estén todos en tu   your house, *sit* in front of the
casa, *siéntense* **frente a la** fireplace and *begin* to tell scary
chimenea y *empiecen* **a contar** stories. Did you understand?
historias de terror. ¿Entendiste?

20 volver   turn; return

type 1 stem-changing verb **o** → **ue**

GERUND	PAST PARTICIPLE
volviendo	vuelto

PRESENT INDICATIVE	PRESENT PERFECT
vuelvo	he vuelto
vuelves	
vuelve	
volvemos	
volvéis	
vuelven	

PRESENT PROGRESSIVE	IMPERFECT PROGRESSIVE
estoy volviendo	estaba volviendo

IMPERFECT INDICATIVE	PRETERITE
volvía	volví

PLUPERFECT	PAST ANTERIOR
había vuelto	hube vuelto

Similar verbs

Only a very small selection of **o** → **ue** stem-changing verbs is listed here.

acordarse	remember	**encontrar**	find, meet
costar	cost	**soler**	be accustomed / used to

Note: These verbs are type 1 stem-changing verbs and are irregular only in the present indicative and present subjunctive tenses and thus also in the imperative forms except the **vosotros** form (**volved**). The **-o-** in the stem changes to **-ue-** in forms where the stress falls on the syllable containing the **-o-**. In forms that have the stress on the ending, the **-o-** remains. Most of these verbs, are in other respects regular, but note, for example, the irregular past participle of **volver** (**vuelto**) and its compound forms, such as **envolver** (**envuelto**) and **resolver** (**resuelto**). All of these verbs are either **-ar** or **-er** verbs and take the regular endings for their group. Note, however, that verbs ending in **-car, -zar,** or **-gar** are also spelling-change verbs: ➤ Model Verbs 5, 6, and 7, respectively.

IMPERATIVE	
(tú) vuelve	(vosotros) volved
(usted) vuelva	(ustedes) vuelvan

FUTURE	**FUTURE PERFECT**
volveré	habré vuelto

CONDITIONAL	**CONDITIONAL PERFECT**
volvería	habría/hubiera vuelto

PRESENT SUBJUNCTIVE	**PERFECT SUBJUNCTIVE**
vuelva	haya vuelto
vuelvas	
vuelva	
volvamos	
volváis	
vuelvan	

IMPERFECT SUBJUNCTIVE	**PLUPERFECT SUBJUNCTIVE**
volviera/volviese	hubiera/hubiese vuelto

La pesadilla

Anoche tuve un sueño extraño. Por lo general no *me acuerdo* de lo que sueño, pero esta vez fue muy sencillo *acordarse*. En el sueño, mi esposa y yo *nos encontramos* en el restaurante donde *solíamos* ir cuando éramos novios. Ella, sin embargo, no *se acordaba* del lugar. Después, me dijo que me *encontraba* extraño. Cuando *volví* la cara hacia el espejo, mis facciones eran distintas a las que *yo solía* tener. ¡Qué terrible!

The nightmare

Last night I had a weird dream. Generally, *I do* not *remember* what I dream, but this time it was easy *to remember*. In the dream, my wife and I *met* at the restaurant where *we used to* go when we were girlfriend and boyfriend. However, *she did* not *remember* the place. Then, she told me *she found* me weird. When *I turned* my face to the mirror, my traits were different from the ones *I used to* have. How terrible!

21 jugar   play; gamble

type 1 stem-changing verb **u** → **ue**

GERUND	PAST PARTICIPLE
jugando	jugado

PRESENT INDICATIVE	PRESENT PERFECT
juego	he jugado
juegas	
juega	
jugamos	
jugáis	
juegan	

PRESENT PROGRESSIVE	IMPERFECT PROGRESSIVE
estoy jugando	estaba jugando

IMPERFECT INDICATIVE	PRETERITE
jugaba	jugué
jugabas	jugaste
jugaba	jugó
jugábamos	jugamos
jugábais	jugasteis
jugaban	jugaron

Note: **Jugar** is the only verb that has the **u** → **ue** spelling change. For all other purposes, it is a member of the type 1 **o** → **ue** family.

What happens with **jugar** is that the -**u**- in the stem changes to -**ue**- in those forms in which the stress falls on the syllable containing -**u**-. In those forms that have the stress on the ending, the -**u**- remains. Since it is only in the present and present subjunctive tenses where some forms have the stress on the stem, this change does not occur in the other tenses.

Note, however, the **u** in the first person singular of the preterite tense and in all the forms of the present subjunctive tense. This is simply to preserve the pronunciation of the hard **g** in those forms where the verb ending begins with an **e**.

IMPERATIVE	
(tú) juega	(vosotros) jugad
(usted) juegue	(ustedes) jueguen

PLUPERFECT	*PAST ANTERIOR*
había jugado	hube jugado
FUTURE	*FUTURE PERFECT*
jugaré	habré jugado
CONDITIONAL	*CONDITIONAL PERFECT*
jugaría	habría/hubiera jugado
PRESENT SUBJUNCTIVE	*PERFECT SUBJUNCTIVE*
juegue	haya jugado
juegues	
juegue	
juguemos	
juguéis	
jueguen	

IMPERFECT SUBJUNCTIVE	*PLUPERFECT SUBJUNCTIVE*
jugara/jugase	hubiera/hubiese jugado

Maradona *juega* otra vez por la selección argentina.	Maradona *plays* again for the Argentinian team.
Los niños que *juegan* en la calle corren grandes riesgos.	Children who *play* in the street run great risks.
No *juegues* todo tu dinero.	*Do*n't *gamble* all your money away.
Si yo fuera más alto, *jugaría* baloncesto.	If I were taller, *I would play* basketball.

type 2 stem-changing verb **e** → **ie** and **i**

GERUND	PAST PARTICIPLE
sintiendo	sentido

PRESENT INDICATIVE	PRESENT PERFECT
siento	he sentido
sientes	
siente	
sentimos	
sentís	
sienten	

PRESENT PROGRESSIVE	IMPERFECT PROGRESSIVE
estoy sintiendo	estaba sintiendo

IMPERFECT INDICATIVE	PRETERITE
sentía	sentí
	sentiste
	sintió
	sentimos
	sentisteis
	sintieron

Similar verbs

advertir	warn, advise	mentir	lie
diferir	differ	preferir	prefer
divertirse	enjoy oneself	referir	refer, relate
herir	wound, hurt	sugerir	suggest

Note: These verbs are type 2 stem-changing verbs and are all **-ir** verbs. They have the change **e** → **ie** in some forms of the present indicative and present subjunctive tenses, and therefore also in the imperative forms except the **vosotros** form (**sentid**). What happens is that the **-e-** in the stem changes to **-ie-** in those forms in which the stress falls on the syllable containing the **-e-**. In those forms that have the stress on the ending, the **-e-** remains. In addition, these verbs have a change from **e** → **i** in the gerund, in the first and second persons plural forms of the present tense, in the third person forms of the preterite tense, and in all forms of the imperfect subjunctive tense. These verbs are regular in other respects.

STEM-CHANGING VERBS　　sentir　22

IMPERATIVE
(tú) siente
(usted) sienta

(vosotros) sentid
(ustedes) sientan

PLUPERFECT
había sentido

PAST ANTERIOR
hube sentido

FUTURE
sentiré

FUTURE PERFECT
habré sentido

CONDITIONAL
sentiría

CONDITIONAL PERFECT
habría / hubiera sentido

PRESENT SUBJUNCTIVE
sienta
sientas
sienta
sintamos
sintáis
sientan

PERFECT SUBJUNCTIVE
haya sentido

IMPERFECT SUBJUNCTIVE
sintiera / sintiese

PLUPERFECT SUBJUNCTIVE
hubiera / hubiese sentido

Un consejo

Está bien que *te diviertas*, pero te *advierto* que es malo pasar todo el tiempo jugando. Te *sugiero* que estudies con tu amiga; si *prefieren*, pueden hacerlo en su casa. Pero por favor no me *mientan*, porque eso *hiere* mis sentimientos.

Some advice

It is fine for *you to have a good time,* but *I warn* you that it is not good to spend all your time playing. *I suggest* that you study with your friend; if *you both prefer*, you can do so at her house. But please *do* not *lie* to me, because that *hurts* my feelings.

23 dormir(se)　　　　sleep; fall asleep

type 2 stem-changing verb **o** → **ue** and **u**

GERUND	PAST PARTICIPLE
durmiendo	dormido

PRESENT INDICATIVE	PRESENT PERFECT
duermo	he dormido
duermes	
duerme	
dormimos	
dormís	
duermen	

PRESENT PROGRESSIVE	IMPERFECT PROGRESSIVE
estoy durmiendo	estaba durmiendo

IMPERFECT INDICATIVE	PRETERITE
dormía	dormí
	dormiste
	durmió
	dormimos
	dormisteis
	durmieron

Similar verb

morir　　　die

Note:　These verbs are type 2 stem-changing verbs. They change from **o** → **ue** in the present indicative and present subjunctive tenses, and therefore also in the imperative forms except the **vosotros** form (**dormid**). What happens is that the **-o-** in the stem changes to **-ue-** in those forms in which the stress falls on the syllable containing the **-o-**. In those forms that have the stress on the ending, the **-o-** remains. In addition, these two verbs change from **o** → **u** in the gerund, in the third person forms of the preterite tense, in all forms of the imperfect subjunctive forms, and in the first and second persons plural forms of the present subjunctive tense. All of these forms, have an ending beginning with an **-i-**. These verbs are regular in other respects, but note the irregular past participle of **morir** (**muerto**).

IMPERATIVE

(tú) duerme

(usted) duerma

(vosotros) dormid

(ustedes) duerman

PLUPERFECT	**PAST ANTERIOR**
había dormido	hube dormido
FUTURE	**FUTURE PERFECT**
dormiré	habré dormido
CONDITIONAL	**CONDITIONAL PERFECT**
dormiría	habría/hubiera dormido
PRESENT SUBJUNCTIVE	**PERFECT SUBJUNCTIVE**
duerma	haya dormido
duermas	
duerma	
durmamos	
durmáis	
duerman	
IMPERFECT SUBJUNCTIVE	**PLUPERFECT SUBJUNCTIVE**
durmiera/durmiese	hubiera/hubiese dormido

Las noticias	The news
CINCO PERSONAS *MURIERON* EN UN ACCIDENTE DE TRÁNSITO	FIVE PERSONS *DIED* IN A CAR ACCIDENT
CHOFER *SE DURMIÓ:* ES UN MILAGRO QUE NADIE *HAYA MUERTO*	DRIVER *FELL ASLEEP:* IT IS A MIRACLE THAT NOBODY *HAS DIED*
HACE UNA SEMANA QUE EL PRESIDENTE NO *DUERME*	IT'S BEEN A WEEK THAT THE PRESIDENT *HASN'T SLEPT*
ENFERMO *MORIRÁ* SI NO CONSIGUE UN DONANTE DE RIÑÓN	SICK MAN *WILL DIE* IF HE DOESN'T GET A KIDNEY DONOR

24 pedir   request, ask for; order

type 3 stem-changing verb **e** → **i**

GERUND	*PAST PARTICIPLE*
pidiendo	pedido

PRESENT INDICATIVE	*PRESENT PERFECT*
pido	he pedido
pides	
pide	
pedimos	
pedís	
piden	

PRESENT PROGRESSIVE	*IMPERFECT PROGRESSIVE*
estoy pidiendo	estaba pidiendo

IMPERFECT INDICATIVE	*PRETERITE*
pedía	pedí
	pediste
	pidió
	pedimos
	pedisteis
	pidieron

Similar verbs

conseguir	manage, get hold of	**reñir**	scold
corregir	correct	**repetir**	repeat
despedir(se)	fire, dismiss; say good-bye to, take leave of	**seguir**	follow, carry on
elegir	elect, choose	**servir**	serve
gemir	groan	**sonreír**	smile
impedir	prevent	**teñir**	dye
regir	rule	**vestir(se)**	dress
reírse	laugh		

(plus any compounds of these verbs)

Note: These verbs, which are all **-ir** verbs, are type 3 stem-changing verbs. Their stems have the spelling change **e** → **i** in most forms of the present indicative tense and in all forms of the present subjunctive tense, and therefore in the imperative forms except for the **vosotros** form (**pedid**). It also occurs in the third person forms of the preterite tense and in all forms of the imperfect subjunctive tense, and in the gerund.

pedir 24

IMPERATIVE
(tú) pide
(usted) pida

(vosotros) pedid
(ustedes) pidan

PLUPERFECT
había pedido

PAST ANTERIOR
hube pedido

FUTURE
pediré

FUTURE PERFECT
habré pedido

CONDITIONAL
pediría

CONDITIONAL PERFECT
habría/hubiera pedido

PRESENT SUBJUNCTIVE
pida
pidas
pida
pidamos
pidáis
pidan

PERFECT SUBJUNCTIVE
haya pedido

IMPERFECT SUBJUNCTIVE
pidiera/pidiese

PLUPERFECT SUBJUNCTIVE
hubiera/hubiese pedido

Pide lo que quieras.

Order whatever you want.

Si me *despidieran*, no podría pagar el alquiler.

If *they fired* me, I wouldn't be able to pay the rent.

Estaban sirviendo la cena cuando sonó la alarma.

They were serving dinner when the alarm went off.

Pediré una bicicleta nueva para Navidad.

I will ask for a new bicycle for Christmas.

No te *habría despedido* si no fueras tan flojo.

*I would*n't *have fired* you if you were not so lazy.

Irregular Verbs

The following are the most common irregular verbs in Spanish. Some of them have a unique spelling change, while others do not conform to a predictable pattern.

In the future and conditional tenses, only the stem can be irregular; the set of endings is always the same. Therefore, only the first person singular form is given. For the full set of endings, see The Complete System of Tenses in Spanish [➤Model Verb 1]. Any irregularity in the future tense stem will apply to the conditional as well.

Except for **ser** and **ir,** the imperfect indicative and subjunctive tenses of all verbs are regular, and either the **-ar** or **-er/-ir** set of endings must be used. Therefore, only the first person singular form is given; the others are easy to work out from the Regular Verbs [➤Model Verbs 2, 3, 4].

Similarly, compound tenses using the auxiliaries **estar** or **haber** are not given in full: for the whole set of forms, consult the tables for **estar** or **haber** [➤Model Verbs 38, 40] or look at The Complete System of Tenses in Spanish [➤Model Verb 1].

Verbs with a **pretérito grave** [➤The Verb System in Spanish, 10b(ix)] are marked (**pg**).

Verbs with present indicative and subjunctive forms that follow the stem-change pattern described in The Verb System in Spanish, 10b(v) [➤Model Verbs 19–24], are marked (**sc**).

GERUND	PAST PARTICIPLE
abriendo	abierto

PRESENT INDICATIVE	PRESENT PERFECT
abro	he abierto
abres	
abre	
abrimos	
abrís	
abren	

PRESENT PROGRESSIVE	IMPERFECT PROGRESSIVE
estoy abriendo	estaba abriendo

IMPERFECT INDICATIVE	PRETERITE
abría	abrí
	abriste
	abrió
	abrimos
	abristeis
	abrieron

Similar verbs

cubrir	cover	**entreabrir**	half open
descubrir	discover, uncover		

Note: The only irregularity lies in the formation of the past participle. In every other respect, these are regular verbs of the **-ir** family.

IMPERATIVE	
(tú) abre	(vosotros) abrid
(usted) abra	(ustedes) abran

PLUPERFECT	*PAST ANTERIOR*
había/abierto	hube/abierto
FUTURE	*FUTURE PERFECT*
abriré	habré abierto
CONDITIONAL	*CONDITIONAL PERFECT*
abriría	habría/hubiera abierto
PRESENT SUBJUNCTIVE	*PERFECT SUBJUNCTIVE*
abra	haya abierto
abras	
abra	
abramos	
abráis	
abran	
IMPERFECT SUBJUNCTIVE	*PLUPERFECT SUBJUNCTIVE*
abriera/abriese	hubiera/hubiese abierto

Unos avisos	**A few notices**
ABIERTO DE 9 A 5	*OPEN* FROM 9 TO 5
ABRA EL GRIFO CON CUIDADO	*TURN* THE FAUCET ON WITH CARE
ESTA PUERTA *SE ABRE* CON TARJETA ELECTRÓNICA SOLAMENTE	THIS DOOR *OPENS* WITH AN ELECTRONIC CARD ONLY
ABRIMOS EL 1° DE SEPTIEMBRE	*WE OPEN* ON SEPTEMBER 1ST
ESTA TIENDA NO *ABRIRÁ* EL PRÓXIMO DOMINGO	THIS STORE *WILL* NOT *OPEN* NEXT SUNDAY

(sc)

GERUND	PAST PARTICIPLE
adquiriendo	adquirido

PRESENT INDICATIVE	PRESENT PERFECT
adquiero	he adquirido
adquieres	
adquiere	
adquirimos	
adquirís	
adquieren	

PRESENT PROGRESSIVE	IMPERFECT PROGRESSIVE
estoy adquiriendo	estaba adquiriendo

IMPERFECT INDICATIVE	PRETERITE
adquiría	adquirí
	adquiriste
	adquirió
	adquirimos
	adquiristeis
	adquirieron

Note: This verb behaves like a stem-changing verb when the stem vowel is stressed; elsewhere, the **-i-** of the infinitive stem remains.

IMPERATIVE	
(tú) adquiere	(vosotros) adquirid
(usted) adquiera	(ustedes) adquieran

PLUPERFECT	*PAST ANTERIOR*
había adquirido	hube adquirido

FUTURE	*FUTURE PERFECT*
adquiriré	habré adquirido

CONDITIONAL	*CONDITIONAL PERFECT*
adquiriría	habría/hubiera adquirido

PRESENT SUBJUNCTIVE	*PERFECT SUBJUNCTIVE*
adquiera	haya adquirido
adquieras	
adquiera	
adquiramos	
adquiráis	
adquieran	

IMPERFECT SUBJUNCTIVE	*PLUPERFECT SUBJUNCTIVE*
adquiriera/adquiriese	hubiera/hubiese adquirido

Habíamos adquirido un auto nuevo, pero tuvimos que devolverlo.

We had purchased a new car, but we had to return it.

Está adquiriendo un departamento a plazos.

He is purchasing an apartment in installments.

Adquirí una gran experiencia gracias a mis viajes por todo el mundo.

I acquired a lot of experience thanks to my trips all around the world.

(pg)

GERUND	PAST PARTICIPLE
andando	andado

PRESENT INDICATIVE	PRESENT PERFECT
ando	he andado
andas	
anda	
andamos	
andáis	
andan	

PRESENT PROGRESSIVE	IMPERFECT PROGRESSIVE
estoy andando	estaba andando

IMPERFECT INDICATIVE	PRETERITE
andaba	anduve
	anduviste
	anduvo
	anduvimos
	anduvisteis
	anduvieron

Note: The preterite forms and consequently the imperfect subjunctive forms (of **pretérito grave** type) are the only irregularities. In every other respect, **andar** behaves like a regular **-ar** verb.

IMPERATIVE

(tú) anda	(vosotros) andad
(usted) ande	(ustedes) anden

PLUPERFECT	*PAST ANTERIOR*
había andado	hube andado
FUTURE	*FUTURE PERFECT*
andaré	habré andado
CONDITIONAL	*CONDITIONAL PERFECT*
andaría	habría/hubiera andado
PRESENT SUBJUNCTIVE	*PERFECT SUBJUNCTIVE*
ande	haya andado
andes	
ande	
andemos	
andéis	
anden	
IMPERFECT SUBJUNCTIVE	*PLUPERFECT SUBJUNCTIVE*
anduviera/anduviese	hubiera/hubiese andado

Dime con quién *andas* y te diré quién eres.	Tell me who *you go around* with and I'll tell you who you are.
Andamos muchas horas antes de encontrar una farmacia.	*We walked* for many hours before finding a drugstore.
Siempre voy *andando* al colegio.	*I* always *walk* to school.
Si no *anduviera* tanto, mi padre estaría muy gordo.	If *he did*n't *walk* so much, my father would be very fat.

(sc + pg)

GERUND	PAST PARTICIPLE
bendiciendo	bendecido

PRESENT INDICATIVE	PRESENT PERFECT
bendigo	he bendecido
bendices	
bendice	
bendecimos	
bendecís	
bendicen	

PRESENT PROGRESSIVE	IMPERFECT PROGRESSIVE
estoy bendiciendo	estaba bendiciendo

IMPERFECT INDICATIVE	PRETERITE
bendecía	bendije
	bendijiste
	bendijo
	bendijimos
	bendijisteis
	bendijeron

PLUPERFECT	PAST ANTERIOR
había bendecido	hube bendecido

Similar verb

maldecir   curse, damn

Note: The key irregularities are:

- the first person singular form of the present tense, and therefore all of the present subjunctive forms take **-g-** in place of **-c-;**
- the present indicative tense, which behaves like a type 3 stem-changing verb;
- the **pretérito grave** and therefore the imperfect subjunctive forms.

In other respects, **bendecir** behaves like a regular **-ir** verb. It largely follows its 'parent' verb, **decir**, with the following exceptions:

- the past participle, which is regular, unlike **decir** (**dicho**);
- the singular familiar imperative, which is regular (unlike **di**);
- the regular formation of the future and conditional stem.

IMPERATIVE

(tú) bendice   (vosotros) bendecid
(usted) bendiga   (ustedes) bendigan

FUTURE   *FUTURE PERFECT*
bendeciré   habré bendecido
bendecirás
bendecirá
bendeciremos
bendeciréis
bendecirán

CONDITIONAL   *CONDITIONAL PERFECT*
bendeciría   habría / hubiera bendecido

PRESENT SUBJUNCTIVE   *PERFECT SUBJUNCTIVE*
bendiga   haya bendecido
bendigas
bendiga
bendigamos
bendigáis
bendigan

IMPERFECT SUBJUNCTIVE   *PLUPERFECT SUBJUNCTIVE*
bendijera / bendijese   hubiera / hubiese bendecido

¡*Bendígame*, Padre, pues he   *Bless me,* Father, for I have
pecado!   sinned!

¡Dios te *bendiga!*   May God *bless* you!

El Papa *bendecirá* la nueva   The Pope *will bless* the new
catedral.   cathedral.

La gente *maldijo* a los soldados The people *damned* the soldiers
que atacaron el templo.   who attacked the temple.

29 caber

fit

(pg)

GERUND	PAST PARTICIPLE
cabiendo	cabido

PRESENT INDICATIVE	PRESENT PERFECT
quepo	he cabido
cabes	
cabe	
cabemos	
cabéis	
caben	

PRESENT PROGRESSIVE	IMPERFECT PROGRESSIVE
estoy cabiendo	estaba cabiendo

IMPERFECT INDICATIVE	PRETERITE
cabía	cupe
	cupiste
	cupo
	cupimos
	cupisteis
	cupieron

Note: The key irregularities are:

• the first person singular form of the present tense, and therefore the present subjunctive tense;
• the **pretérito grave** and therefore the imperfect subjunctive tense;
• the future tense stem.

IMPERATIVE
(tú) cabe
(usted) quepa

(vosotros) cabed
(ustedes) quepan

PLUPERFECT
había cabido

PAST ANTERIOR
hube cabido

FUTURE
cabré

FUTURE PERFECT
habré cabido

CONDITIONAL
cabría

CONDITIONAL PERFECT
habría/hubiera cabido

PRESENT SUBJUNCTIVE
quepa
quepas
quepa
quepamos
quepáis
quepan

PERFECT SUBJUNCTIVE
haya cabido

IMPERFECT SUBJUNCTIVE
cupiera/cupiese

PLUPERFECT SUBJUNCTIVE
hubiera/hubiese cabido

¡El auto es muy pequeño, no *cabremos* todos!

The car is very small, *we will* not all *fit*!

Si quieres que *quepan* todos los muebles, debemos ampliar la casa.

If you want all the furniture *to fit*, we must expand the house.

GERUND	PAST PARTICIPLE
cayendo	caído

PRESENT INDICATIVE	PRESENT PERFECT
caigo	he caído
caes	
cae	
caemos	
caéis	
caen	

PRESENT PROGRESSIVE	IMPERFECT PROGRESSIVE
estoy cayendo	estaba cayendo

IMPERFECT INDICATIVE	PRETERITE
caía	caí
	caíste
	cayó
	caímos
	caísteis
	cayeron

Similar verb

decaer　　　decay, decline

Note:　　The key irregularities are:

　　　• the first person singular form of the present indicative tense and so all forms of the present subjunctive tense are based on the stem **caig-**;
　　　• a **-y-** is needed in the third person forms of the preterite tense;
　　　• an accent is needed on the **-i-** when it is stressed.

　　　The verbs **roer** (gnaw) and **corroer** (corrode) follow a largely similar pattern.

IRREGULAR VERBS   caer(se) 30

IMPERATIVE
(tú) cae
(usted) caiga

(vosotros) caed
(ustedes) caigan

PLUPERFECT
había caído

PAST ANTERIOR
hube caído

FUTURE
caeré

FUTURE PERFECT
habré caido

CONDITIONAL
caería

CONDITIONAL PERFECT
habría/hubiera caído

PRESENT SUBJUNCTIVE
caiga
caigas
caiga
caigamos
caigáis
caigan

PLUPERFECT SUBJUNCTIVE
haya caído

IMPERFECT SUBJUNCTIVE
cayera/cayese

PLUPERFECT SUBJUNCTIVE
hubiera/hubiese caído

¡Ten cuidado, o *te caerás*!   Be careful or *you will fall*!

Se cayó en un hoyo enorme.   *He fell* into a huge hole.

¡*Caed* de rodillas!   *Fall* on your knees!

31 conducir   drive; lead; conduct

(pg)

GERUND	PAST PARTICIPLE
conduciendo	conducido

PRESENT INDICATIVE	PRESENT PERFECT
conduzco	he conducido
conduces	
conduce	
conducimos	
conducís	
conducen	

PRESENT PROGRESSIVE	IMPERFECT PROGRESSIVE
estoy conduciendo	estaba conduciendo

IMPERFECT INDICATIVE	PRETERITE
conducía	conduje
	condujiste
	condujo
	condujimos
	condujisteis
	condujeron

Similar verbs

All verbs ending in **-ducir**:

aducir	adduce	**producir**	produce, generate, yield
deducir	deduce	**reducir**	lower, reduce, shorten
inducir	induce	**reproducir**	reproduce
introducir	introduce, bring in, insert	**traducir**	translate

Note: The key irregularities are:

• the first person singular form of the present tense, and therefore all of the present subjunctive forms take **-zc-** in place of **-c-**;
• the **pretérito grave** and therefore the imperfect subjunctive tense.

IMPERATIVE
(tú) conduce
(usted) conduzca
(vosotros) conducid
(ustedes) conduzcan

PLUPERFECT
había conducido

PAST ANTERIOR
hube conducido

FUTURE
conduciré

FUTURE PERFECT
habré conducido

CONDITIONAL
conduciría

CONDITIONAL PERFECT
habría/hubiera conducido

PRESENT SUBJUNCTIVE
conduzca
conduzcas
conduzca
conduzcamos
conduzcáis
conduzcan

PERFECT SUBJUNCTIVE
haya conducido

IMPERFECT SUBJUNCTIVE
condujera/condujese

PLUPERFECT SUBJUNCTIVE
hubiera/hubiese conducido

El profesor *tradujo* la carta.	The teacher *translated* the letter.
Introduzca una moneda.	*Insert* a coin.
El chofer *conducía* muy de prisa.	The driver *drove* very fast.
Si no me lo decías, lo *hubiera deducido* de todos modos.	If you didn't tell me, *I would have deduced* it anyway.

32 conocer   know; get to know; meet

GERUND	PAST PARTICIPLE
conociendo	conocido

PRESENT INDICATIVE	PRESENT PERFECT
conozco	he conocido
conoces	
conoce	
conocemos	
conocéis	
conocen	

PRESENT PROGRESSIVE	IMPERFECT PROGRESSIVE
estoy conociendo	estaba conociendo

IMPERFECT INDICATIVE	PRETERITE
conocía	conocí
	conociste
	conoció
	conocimos
	conocisteis
	conocieron

Similar verbs

abastecer	provide, supply	embellecer	embellish, beautify
aborrecer	hate, abhor	encanecer	go gray
acontecer	happen, occur	endurecer(se)	harden
agradecer	thank	enfurecer	enrage, madden
amanecer	dawn	enloquecer	madden
anochecer	get dark	enriquecer(se)	enrich
aparecer	appear	ensordecer	deafen
apetecer	feel like, want	entristecer	sadden
carecer	lack	envejecer	age
compadecer	pity, sympathize	envilecer	degrade
crecer	grow	esclarecer	clear up
desaparecer	disappear	establecer	establish, set up
desconocer	not know	estremecerse	quiver, shiver
desobedecer	disobey	favorecer	favor

IMPERATIVE

(tú) conoce	(vosotros) conoced
(usted) conozca	(ustedes) conozcan

PLUPERFECT
había conocido

PAST ANTERIOR
hube conocido

FUTURE
conoceré

FUTURE PERFECT
habré conocido

CONDITIONAL
conocería

CONDITIONAL PERFECT
habría/hubiera conocido

PRESENT SUBJUNCTIVE
conozca
conozcas
conozca
conozcamos
conozcáis
conozcan

PERFECT SUBJUNCTIVE
haya conocido

IMPERFECT SUBJUNCTIVE
conociera/conociese

PLUPERFECT SUBJUNCTIVE
hubiera/hubiese conocido

---

florecer	flourish, flower, bloom	**oscurecer**	grow dark
fortalecer	strengthen	**padecer**	suffer
humedecer	dampen, moisten	**palidecer**	turn pale
languidecer	languish, pine (away)	**parecer**	appear, seem
merecer	deserve	**pertenecer**	belong
nacer	be born	**reconocer**	acknowledge, recognize

Note: The only irregularities are the first person singular form of the present indicative tense, and in consequence all forms of the present subjunctive tense.

Nos *conocimos* en Madrid.   *We met* in Madrid.

Los niños *crecen* rápidamente.   Children *grow* quickly.

El hombre *desapareció* al final de la calle.   The man *disappeared* at the end of the street.

GERUND	PAST PARTICIPLE
dando	dado

PRESENT INDICATIVE	PRESENT PERFECT
doy	he dado
das	
da	
damos	
dais	
dan	

PRESENT PROGRESSIVE	IMPERFECT PROGRESSIVE
estoy dando	estaba dando

IMPERFECT INDICATIVE	PRETERITE
daba	di
	diste
	dio
	dimos
	disteis
	dieron

Note: The key irregularities are:

- the first person singular form of the present tense, ending in **-oy;**
- the accent on the form **dé,** needed to distinguish it from the preposition **de;**
- the preterite forms, in which **dar** behaves like an **-er/-ir** verb, and needs no written accents;
- the imperfect subjunctive forms, based on the preterite stem.

IMPERATIVE
(tú) da
(usted) dé

(vosotros) dad
(ustedes) den

PLUPERFECT
había dado

PAST ANTERIOR
hube dado

FUTURE
daré

FUTURE PERFECT
habré dado

CONDITIONAL
daría

CONDITIONAL PERFECT
habría/hubiera dado

PRESENT SUBJUNCTIVE
dé
des
dé
demos
deis
den

PERFECT SUBJUNCTIVE
haya dado

IMPERFECT SUBJUNCTIVE
diera/diese

PLUPERFECT SUBJUNCTIVE
hubiera/hubiese dado

Mi padre me *dio* sólo cien pesos.

My father *gave* me only a hundred pesos.

Dame todo lo que tienes.

Give me everything you have.

Hubiera dado todo lo que tengo por conocerte antes.

I'd have given everything I have to have met you before.

El gobierno *dará* alimentos a las personas desempleadas.

The government *will give* food to unemployed people.

34 decir   say; tell

(sc + pg)

GERUND	PAST PARTICIPLE
diciendo	dicho

PRESENT INDICATIVE	PRESENT PERFECT
digo	he dicho
dices	
dice	
decimos	
decís	
dicen	

PRESENT PROGRESSIVE	IMPERFECT PROGRESSIVE
estoy diciendo	estaba diciendo

IMPERFECT INDICATIVE	PRETERITE
decía	dije
	dijiste
	dijo
	dijimos
	dijisteis
	dijeron

Similar verbs

contradecir(se)	contradict (oneself)	**predecir**	predict
desdecir(se)	clash with, withdraw		

Note: The key irregularities are:

- the first person singular form of the present tense, and therefore all forms of the present subjunctive tense, take **-g-** in place of **-c-;**
- the present indicative tense, which behaves like a type 3 stem-changing verb;
- the **pretérito grave,** and therefore the imperfect subjunctive forms;
- the past participle forms, similar to those of **hacer** (**hecho**);
- the future and conditional stem, **dir-**.

IMPERATIVE	
(tú) di	(vosotros) decid
(usted) diga	(ustedes) digan

PLUPERFECT	*PAST ANTERIOR*
había dicho	hube dicho

FUTURE	*FUTURE PERFECT*
diré	habré dicho

CONDITIONAL	*CONDITIONAL PERFECT*
diría	habría/hubiera dicho

PRESENT SUBJUNCTIVE	*PERFECT SUBJUNCTIVE*
diga	haya dicho
digas	
diga	
digamos	
digáis	
digan	

IMPERFECT SUBJUNCTIVE	*PLUPERFECT SUBJUNCTIVE*
dijera/dijese	hubiera/hubiese dicho

¡*Dicho* y hecho!	No sooner *said* than done!
¡*Dicen* que es loco!	*They say* he's crazy!
***Digan* lo que *digan*...**	Whatever *they say* . . .
El adivino no *predijo* lo que le iba a pasar.	The fortune-teller *did*n't *predict* what was going to happen to him.
Estoy *diciendo* todo lo que sé.	*I am telling* everything I know.
No te *contradigas*.	*Do* not *contradict* yourself.
El ministro *se desdijo* de sus anteriores declaraciones.	The minister *withdrew* from his previous statements.

35 erguir(se)   raise; lift; straighten up

GERUND	*PAST PARTICIPLE*
irguiendo	erguido

PRESENT INDICATIVE	*PRESENT PERFECT*
yergo/irgo	he erguido
yergues/irgues	
yergue/irgue	
erguimos	
erguís	
yerguen/irguen	

PRESENT PROGRESSIVE	*IMPERFECT PROGRESSIVE*
estoy irguiendo	estaba irguiendo

IMPERFECT INDICATIVE	*PRETERITE*
erguía	erguí
	erguiste
	irguió
	erguimos
	erguisteis
	irguieron

Note: This verb has three possible stems, and in some forms two alternative forms exist. The **ye-** stem is basically due to this verb being a stem-changing verb: instead of beginning with **ie-,** however, stressed-stem forms begin with **ye-**. Note the **-u-** needed in all forms in which the verb ending begins with an **-e**. The one regular feature of this verb is that all its endings follow the pattern for a regular **-ir** verb [▶**vivir** 4].

IMPERATIVE
(tú) yergue/irgue
(usted) yerga/irga

(vosotros) erguid
(ustedes) yergan/irgan

PLUPERFECT
había erguido

PAST ANTERIOR
hube erguido

FUTURE
erguiré

FUTURE PERFECT
habré erguido

CONDITIONAL
erguiría

CONDITIONAL PERFECT
habría/hubiera erguido

PRESENT SUBJUNCTIVE
yerga/irga
yergas/irgas
yerga/irga
yergamos/irgamos
yergáis/irgáis
yergan/irgan

PERFECT SUBJUNCTIVE
haya erguido

IMPERFECT SUBJUNCTIVE
irguiera/irguiese

PLUPERFECT SUBJUNCTIVE
hubiera/hubiese erguido

¡Ponte **erguido**!

La torre *se yergue* sobre la ciudad.

Los soldados *se irguieron* cuando entró el general.

Straighten up!

The tower *rises* over the city.

The soldiers *straightened up* when the general came in.

(sc)

GERUND	PAST PARTICIPLE
errando	errado

PRESENT INDICATIVE	PRESENT PERFECT
yerro	he errado
yerras	
yerra	
erramos	
erráis	
yerran	

PRESENT PROGRESSIVE	IMPERFECT PROGRESSIVE
estoy errando	estaba errando

IMPERFECT INDICATIVE	PRETERITE
erraba	erré
	erraste
	erró
	erramos
	errasteis
	erraron

Note: This verb is basically a stem-changing **-ar** verb. However, the stressed-stem forms begin with **ye-,** rather than with **ie-**. In forms where the stem is unstressed, the **err-** remains. All endings are those of a regular **-ar** verb.

IMPERATIVE
(tú) yerra   (vosotros) errad
(usted) yerre   (ustedes) yerren

PLUPERFECT	**PAST ANTERIOR**
había errado	hube errado

FUTURE   **FUTURE PERFECT**
erraré   habré errado

CONDITIONAL   **CONDITIONAL PERFECT**
erraría   habría/hubiera errado

PRESENT SUBJUNCTIVE   **PERFECT SUBJUNCTIVE**
yerre   haya errado
yerres
yerre
erremos
erréis
yerren

IMPERFECT SUBJUNCTIVE   **PLUPERFECT SUBJUNCTIVE**
errara/errase   hubiera/hubiese errado

Estamos errando por lugares inexplorados.   *We are wandering* by unexplored sites.

Erré muchas veces antes de acertar.   *I erred* many times before scoring.

GERUND	PAST PARTICIPLE
escribiendo	escrito

PRESENT INDICATIVE	PRESENT PERFECT
escribo	he escrito
escribes	
escribe	
escribimos	
escribís	
escriben	

PRESENT PROGRESSIVE	IMPERFECT PROGRESSIVE
estoy escribiendo	estaba escribiendo

IMPERFECT INDICATIVE	PRETERITE
escribía	escribí
	escribiste
	escribió
	escribimos
	escribiste
	escribieron

Similar verbs

describir	describe	**suscribir**	subscribe
inscribir	inscribe, enroll	**transcribir**	transcribe
proscribir	proscribe		

Note: The only irregularity of this verb is its past participle, **escrito**.

IMPERATIVE
(tú) escribe
(usted) escriba

(vosotros) escribid
(ustedes) escriban

PLUPERFECT
había escrito

PAST ANTERIOR
hube escrito

FUTURE
escribiré

FUTURE PERFECT
habré escrito

CONDITIONAL
escribiría

CONDITIONAL PERFECT
habría/hubiera escrito

PRESENT SUBJUNCTIVE
escriba
escribas
escriba
escribamos
escribáis
escriban

PERFECT SUBJUNCTIVE
haya escrito

IMPERFECT SUBJUNCTIVE
escribiera/escribiese

PLUPERFECT SUBJUNCTIVE
hubiera/hubiese escrito

¡*Escríbeme* pronto!

Write to me soon!

Nuestros amigos nos *han escrito* **desde México.**

Our friends *have written* to us from Mexico.

El alcalde *ha proscrito* **las apuestas.**

The mayor *has proscribed* gambling.

El periodista *está transcribiendo* **la entrevista.**

The journalist *is transcribing* the interview.

38 estar   be

(pg)

GERUND	PAST PARTICIPLE
estando	estado

PRESENT INDICATIVE	PRESENT PERFECT
estoy	he estado
estás	
está	
estamos	
estáis	
están	

PRESENT PROGRESSIVE	IMPERFECT PROGRESSIVE
(not used)	(not used)

IMPERFECT INDICATIVE	PRETERITE
estaba	estuve
	estuviste
	estuvo
	estuvimos
	estuvisteis
	estuvieron

Note: This verb looks very much like a regular **-ar** verb, and in many tenses it behaves like one. However, it has some irregular features:

• all forms of the present indicative, the present subjunctive, and the imperative tenses have the stress on the (first) vowel of the ending, and so most forms need a written accent. Note the first person singular form of the present indicative, **estoy;**
• the preterite is a typical **pretérito grave** type, and its stem is also used for the imperfect subjunctive tense.

This verb corresponds to the following uses of the verb *to be:*
• to refer to place or location;
• to refer to the state or condition of somebody or something;
• to describe a state resulting from an action or event;
• to form the present progressive and imperfect progressive tenses.
[➤Berlitz *Spanish Grammar Handbook* for full treatment.]

IMPERATIVE	
(tú) está / estate	(vosotros) estad
(usted) esté	(ustedes) estén

PLUPERFECT	*PAST ANTERIOR*
había estado	hube estado

FUTURE	*FUTURE PERFECT*
estaré	habré estado

CONDITIONAL	*CONDITIONAL PERFECT*
estaría	habría / hubiera estado

PRESENT SUBJUNCTIVE	*PERFECT SUBJUNCTIVE*
esté	haya estado
estés	
esté	
estemos	
estéis	
estén	

IMPERFECT SUBJUNCTIVE	*PLUPERFECT SUBJUNCTIVE*
estuviera / estuviese	hubiera / hubiese estado

¿Dónde *está* tu madre?	Where *is* your mother?
***Estuvimos* allí el año pasado.**	*We were* there last year.
Estábamos *viendo* la televisión cuando llamaste.	*We were watching* television when you called.
Iría si no *estuviera* tan cansado.	I would go if *I were* not so tired.
El libro *estará* listo la próxima semana.	The book *will be* ready next week.

GERUND	PAST PARTICIPLE
friendo	frito

PRESENT INDICATIVE	PRESENT PERFECT
frío	he frito
fríes	
fríe	
freímos	
freís	
fríen	

PRESENT PROGRESSIVE	IMPERFECT PROGRESSIVE
estoy friendo	estaba friendo

IMPERFECT INDICATIVE	PRETERITE
freía	freí
	freíste
	frió
	freímos
	freísteis
	frieron

Note: This verb is largely a type 3 stem-changing verb, but it has the following additional irregularities:

- the accent needed whenever the **-i-** is stressed;
- its past participle.

IMPERATIVE

(tú) fríe

(usted) fría

(vosotros) freíd

(ustedes) frían

PLUPERFECT

había frito

PAST ANTERIOR

hube frito

FUTURE

freiré

FUTURE PERFECT

habré frito

CONDITIONAL

freiría

CONDITIONAL PERFECT

habría/hubiera frito

PRESENT SUBJUNCTIVE

fría

fríos

fría

friamos

friais

frían

PERFECT SUBJUNCTIVE

haya frito

IMPERFECT SUBJUNCTIVE

friera/friese

PLUPERFECT SUBJUNCTIVE

hubiera/hubiese frito

Receta: pescado frito

Lava y corta el pescado en filetes. *Fríelo* **en una sartén grande. Cuando lo** *estés friendo,* **añade sal y pimienta. No lo** *frías* **mucho tiempo. Después que lo** *hayas frito,* **cómelo de inmediato. Si** *freiste* **demasiado pescado, guarda el resto en la refrigeradora.**

Recipe: *fried* fish

Wash the fish and cut it into fillets. *Fry it* in a large frying pan. When *you are frying* it, add salt and pepper. *Don't fry* it for very long. After *you have fried* it, eat it immediately. If *you fried* too much fish, keep it in the refrigerator.

(pg)

GERUND	PAST PARTICIPLE
habiendo	habido

PRESENT INDICATIVE	PRESENT PERFECT*
he	ha habido
has	
ha	
hemos	
habéis	
han	
(hay = there is/are/there)	

PRESENT PROGRESSIVE*	IMPERFECT PROGRESSIVE*
está habiendo	estaba habiendo

IMPERFECT INDICATIVE	PRETERITE
había	hube
	hubiste
	hubo
	hubimos
	hubisteis
	hubieron

Note: This verb is irregular in the following respects:

• the form **hay** is used for *'there is,' 'there are'*; in other tenses the normal third person singular form is used for *'there was,' 'there were'*; etc.;
• this verb has a **pretérito grave,** with **hub-** as its stem. This is also used in the imperfect subjunctive forms;
• the future tense stem is irregular: **habr-;**
• the present subjunctive tense is very irregular, with the stem **hay-;**
• this verb is the one and only auxiliary verb used in Spanish for the following compound tenses: present perfect, pluperfect, past anterior, future perfect, conditional perfect, perfect subjunctive, and pluperfect subjunctive.

IMPERATIVE
(not used)

PLUPERFECT*	*PAST ANTERIOR**
había habido	hubo habido
FUTURE	*FUTURE PERFECT**
habré	habrá habido
CONDITIONAL	*CONDITIONAL PERFECT**
habría	habría/hubiera habido
PRESENT SUBJUNCTIVE	*PERFECT SUBJUNCTIVE**
haya	haya habido
hayas	
haya	
hayamos	
hayáis	
hayan	
IMPERFECT SUBJUNCTIVE	*PLUPERFECT SUBJUNCTIVE**
hubiera/hublese	hubiera/hubiese habido

De postre, *hay* fruta fresca.	For dessert *there's* fresh fruit.
¡Vamos, de prisa, *ha habido* un accidente!	Let's go, quickly, *there has been* an accident!
Mis amigos *han llegado.*	My friends *have arrived.*
***Habíamos pagado* mil pesos.**	*We had paid* a thousand pesos.

* Used only in the third person singular.

41 hacer   do; make

(pg)

GERUND	PAST PARTICIPLE
haciendo	hecho

PRESENT INDICATIVE	PRESENT PERFECT
hago	he hecho
haces	
hace	
hacemos	
hacéis	
hacen	

PRESENT PROGRESSIVE	IMPERFECT PROGRESSIVE
estoy haciendo	estaba haciendo

IMPERFECT INDICATIVE	PRETERITE
hacía	hice
	hiciste
	hizo
	hicimos
	hicisteis
	hicieron

Similar verbs

contrahacer	copy, imitate	**rehacer**	redo, remake
deshacer	undo, ruin	**satisfacer**	satisfy

Note: This verb is irregular in the following respects:

- it has a **pretérito grave**, with **hic-** as its stem (but note **hizo**: the **-c-** changes to **-z-** to keep the sound the same in front of the **-o**). This stem **hic-** is also used in the imperfect subjunctive forms;
- the future tense stem is irregular: **har-**;
- the first person singular form of the present tense has the stem **hag-**, and it is used throughout the present subjunctive tense;
- the past participle is irregular (**hecho**).

IMPERATIVE
(tú) haz   (vosotros) haced
(usted) haga   (ustedes) hagan

PLUPERFECT   *PAST ANTERIOR*
había hecho   hube hecho

FUTURE   *FUTURE PERFECT*
haré   habré hecho

CONDITIONAL   *CONDITIONAL PERFECT*
haría   habría/hubiera hecho

PRESENT SUBJUNCTIVE   *PERFECT SUBJUNCTIVE*
haga   haya hecho
hagas
haga
hagamos
hagáis
hagan

IMPERFECT SUBJUNCTIVE   *PLUPERFECT SUBJUNCTIVE*
hiciera/hiciese   hubiera/hubiese hecho

¿*Estás satisfecho?*   *Are you satisfied?*

¿Qué *hacías* cuando te llamé   What *were you doing* when
anoche?   I called you last night?

¡*Hagan* sus deberes!   *Do* your homework!

Hazme un gran favor: ¡cállate! *Do me* a big favor: Shut up!

¡Mira lo que *has hecho*!   Look at what *you have done*!

Las máquinas *están haciendo*   The machines *are making* too
mucho ruido.   much noise.

GERUND	PAST PARTICIPLE
yendo	ido

PRESENT INDICATIVE	PRESENT PERFECT
voy	he ido
vas	
va	
vamos	
vais	
van	

PRESENT PROGRESSIVE	IMPERFECT PROGRESSIVE
estoy yendo	estaba yendo

IMPERFECT INDICATIVE	PRETERITE
iba	fui
ibas	fuiste
iba	fue
íbamos	fuimos
ibais	fuisteis
iban	fueron

Note: A highly irregular verb, although its endings are often very similar to, or even the same as, most regular verbs. The first step in mastering this verb is to be able to recognize and use correctly the various different stems. The future and conditional tenses and the past participle are regular. Other major features of this verb are:

• present indicative stem **v-** with **-ar** type endings; note first person singular form (**voy**);
• present subjunctive stem **vay-**;
• irregular imperfect indicative tense, but similar to **-ar** verb pattern;
• preterite and imperfect subjunctive forms based on the stem **fu-**; both sets of forms being shared with the verb **ser**.

Note that this verb is used to form the future immediate: e.g., **Mañana vamos a ir de compras** (Tomorrow we are going to go shopping).

IMPERATIVE	
(tú) ve	(vosotros) id
(usted) vaya	(ustedes) vayan

PLUPERFECT	PAST ANTERIOR
había ido	hube ido

FUTURE	FUTURE PERFECT
iré	habré ido

CONDITIONAL	CONDITIONAL PERFECT
iría	habría/hubiera ido

PRESENT SUBJUNCTIVE	PLUPERFECT SUBJUNCTIVE
vaya	haya ido
vayas	
vaya	
vayamos	
vayáis	
vayan	

IMPERFECT SUBJUNCTIVE	PERFECT SUBJUNCTIVE
fuera/fuese	hubiera/hubiese ido

¡Vamos *de vacaciones!*

Niños, mañana *vamos* de vacaciones. La semana pasada, papá *fue a* comprar los billetes. Ahora mismo *voy a* hacer las maletas, y papá *va a* llegar a casa pronto. Y ahora, chicos, *vayan a* bañarse, y María, *vete a* la cama ya; *vamos a* tener que levantarnos temprano.

We're going on vacation!

Children, tomorrow *we are going* on vacation. Last week, Dad *went to* buy the tickets. *I'm* just *about to* pack the suitcases, and Dad *is going to* be home soon. Now, boys, *go* and take a bath, and Maria, *go to* bed now; *we are going to* have to get up early.

GERUND	PAST PARTICIPLE
luciendo	lucido

PRESENT INDICATIVE	PRESENT PERFECT
luzco	he lucido
luces	
luce	
lucimos	
lucís	
lucen	

PRESENT PROGRESSIVE	IMPERFECT PROGRESSIVE
estoy luciendo	estaba luciendo

IMPERFECT INDICATIVE	PRETERITE
lucía	lucí
	luciste
	lució
	lucimos
	lucisteis
	lucieron

Similar verb

relucir　　gleam, shine

Note:　This verb and its compound **relucir** behave very much like **conducir** and its family, except that they do not have a **pretérito grave**. Thus, the first person singular form of the present indicative tense and all forms of the present subjunctive tense have the stem **luzc-**.

IMPERATIVE	
(tú) luce	(vosotros) lucid
(usted) luzca	(ustedes) luzcan

PLUPERFECT	*PAST ANTERIOR*
había lucido	hube lucido

FUTURE	*FUTURE PERFECT*
luciré	habré lucido

CONDITIONAL	*CONDITIONAL PERFECT*
luciría	habría/hubiera lucido

PRESENT SUBJUNCTIVE	*PERFECT SUBJUNCTIVE*
luzca	haya lucido
luzcas	
luzca	
luzcamos	
luzcáis	
luzcan	

IMPERFECT SUBJUNCTIVE	*PLUPERFECT SUBJUNCTIVE*
luciera/luciese	hubiera/hubiese lucido

Miles de estrellas *lucen* en el cielo de Sevilla.	Thousands of stars *shine* in the sky of Seville.
Mi amiga *lució* su vestido nuevo en la fiesta.	My girlfriend *showed off* her new dress at the party.
Mis alumnos *se lucieron* en el concurso de matemáticas.	My students *excelled* in the math contest.

44 oír   hear; listen; pay attention

GERUND	PAST PARTICIPLE
oyendo	oído

PRESENT INDICATIVE	PRESENT PERFECT
oigo	he oído
oyes	
oye	
oímos	
oís	
oyen	

PRESENT PROGRESSIVE	IMPERFECT PROGRESSIVE
estoy oyendo	estaba oyendo

IMPERFECT INDICATIVE	PRETERITE
oía	oí
	oíste
	oyó
	oímos
	oísteis
	oyeron

Similar verb

desoír   ignore, turn a deaf ear to

Note: The key irregularities are:

- the **-i-** of the stem takes an accent when stressed (notice that it is not stressed in **oiga,** the present subjunctive, the future, or the conditional tenses);
- forms with an ending beginning with **-e-** take a **-y-** to avoid three vowels coming together;
- the first person singular form of the present indicative tense has a **-g-,** which is carried into all forms of the present subjunctive tense.

IMPERATIVE
(tú) oye
(usted) oiga

(vosotros) oíd
(ustedes) oigan

PLUPERFECT
había oído

PAST ANTERIOR
hube oído

FUTURE
oiré

FUTURE PERFECT
habré oído

CONDITIONAL
oiría

CONDITIONAL PERFECT
habría/hubiera oído

PRESENT SUBJUNCTIVE
oiga
oigas
oiga
oigamos
oigáis
oigan

PERFECT SUBJUNCTIVE
haya oído

IMPERFECT SUBJUNCTIVE
oyera/oyese

PLUPERFECT SUBJUNCTIVE
hubiera/hubiese oido

¡Habla más fuerte, no te *oigo*! Speak up, *I* can't *hear* you!

***Oiga* usted: ¡no debe hacer eso!** *Listen*, you musn't do that!

Si me *hubieses oído*, no tendrías este problema. If *you had listened to* me, you wouldn't have this problem.

¿*Estás oyendo* las noticias? *Are you listening to* the news?

No *desoigas* un buen consejo. Don't *ignore* a good piece of advice.

GERUND	*PAST PARTICIPLE*
oliendo	olido

PRESENT INDICATIVE	*PRESENT PERFECT*
huelo	he olido
hueles	
huele	
olemos	
oléis	
huelen	

PRESENT PROGRESSIVE	*IMPERFECT PROGRESSIVE*
estoy oliendo	estaba oliendo

IMPERFECT INDICATIVE	*PRETERITE*
olía	olí
	oliste
	olió
	olimos
	olisteis
	olieron

Note: **Oler** is a predictable type 1 stem-changing verb with a particular oddity: the **o-** changes to **-ue-** when the stem is stressed, but the **-ue-** is always preceded by **h-**; then, forms in which the stem is stressed begin with **hue-**. In other respects it is a normal stem-changing verb.

IMPERATIVE
(tú) huele   (vosotros) oled
(usted) huela   (ustedes) huelan

PLUPERFECT   *PAST ANTERIOR*
había olido   hube olido

FUTURE   *FUTURE PERFECT*
oleré   habré olido

CONDITIONAL   *CONDITIONAL PERFECT*
olería   habría / hubiera olido

PRESENT SUBJUNCTIVE   *PERFECT SUBJUNCTIVE*
huela   haya olido
huelas
huela
olamos
oláis
huelan

IMPERFECT SUBJUNCTIVE   *PLUPERFECT SUBJUNCTIVE*
oliera / oliese   hubiera / hubiese olido

Este pastel *huele* a quemado.	This cake *smells* burnt.
¡Qué bien *huelen* estas manzanas!	These apples *smell* so good!
La habitación *olía* a jazmín.	The room *smelled* of jasmine.
De repente, los perros *olieron* el zorro.	Suddenly, the dogs *smelled* the fox.
Muchachos, ¡*huelan* esto! Parece estar podrido.	Boys, *smell* this! It seems to be rotten.

be able to; can; may

(pg)

GERUND	*PAST PARTICIPLE*
pudiendo	podido

PRESENT INDICATIVE	*PRESENT PERFECT*
puedo	he podido
puedes	
puede	
podemos	
podéis	
pueden	

PRESENT PROGRESSIVE	*IMPERFECT PROGRESSIVE*
estoy pudiendo	estaba pudiendo

IMPERFECT INDICATIVE	*PRETERITE*
podía	pude
	pudiste
	pudo
	pudimos
	pudisteis
	pudieron

Note: This verb has the following irregularities:

• the stem changes in the present indicative and subjunctive tenses are those of a type 1 **o** → **e** stem-changing verb;
• this is a **pretérito grave** verb, with the stem **pud-,** which is carried over into the imperfect subjunctive forms:
• in addition, the gerund is **pudiendo**;
• the future and conditional stem loses the **-e-** of the infinitive, becoming **podr-**.

IMPERATIVE
(not used)

PLUPERFECT
había podido

FUTURE
podré

CONDITIONAL
podría

PRESENT SUBJUNCTIVE
pueda
puedas
pueda
podamos
podáis
puedan

IMPERFECT SUBJUNCTIVE
pudiera/pudiese

PAST ANTERIOR
hube podido

FUTURE PERFECT
habré podido

CONDITIONAL PERFECT
habría/hubiera podido

PERFECT SUBJUNCTIVE
haya podido

PLUPERFECT SUBJUNCTIVE
hubiera/hubiese podido

¿*Se puede* telefonear de aquí?

Los alpinistas *no pudieron* llegar hasta la cima porque nevó.

¡No *podría* vivir sin ti!

Mañana *podréis* ver el mar por primera vez.

Aunque *pueda*, no iré.

Can one telephone from here?

The mountaineers *were unable* to get to the top because it snowed.

*I could*n't live without you!

Tomorrow *you will be able to* see the sea for the first time.

Even if *I can*, I won't go.

(pg)

GERUND	PAST PARTICIPLE
poniendo	puesto

PRESENT INDICATIVE	PRESENT PERFECT
pongo	he puesto
pones	
pone	
ponemos	
ponéis	
ponen	

PRESENT PROGRESSIVE	IMPERFECT PROGRESSIVE
estoy poniendo	estaba poniendo

IMPERFECT INDICATIVE	PRETERITE
ponía	puse
	pusiste
	puso
	pusimos
	pusisteis
	pusieron

Similar verbs

componer	compose, fix	**oponer(se)**	oppose,
descomponer	break down,		stand out against
	decompose	**posponer**	postpone
disponer	dispose of,	**proponer**	propose
	have available	**reponerse**	get fit, recover
imponer	impose	**suponer**	suppose
indisponer	indispose	**trasponer**	transpose

Note: This highly irregular verb has the following features:

• the first person singular form of the present tense, and therefore all forms of the present subjunctive tense have the stem **pong-**;
• the preterite is **pretérito grave**, with the stem **pus-**, which is also used in the imperfect subjunctive forms;
• the past participle is irregular (**puesto**);
• the singular informal imperative is **pon**;
• the stem for the future and conditional tenses is **pondr-**.

IMPERATIVE

(tú) pon   (vosotros) poned
(usted) ponga   (ustedes) pongan

PLUPERFECT   *PAST ANTERIOR*
había puesto   hube puesto

FUTURE   *FUTURE PERFECT*
pondré   habré puesto

CONDITIONAL   *CONDITIONAL PERFECT*
pondría   habría/hubiera puesto

PRESENT SUBJUNCTIVE   *PERFECT SUBJUNCTIVE*
ponga   haya puesto
pongas
ponga
pongamos
pongáis
pongan

IMPERFECT SUBJUNCTIVE   *PLUPERFECT SUBJUNCTIVE*
pusiera/pusiese   hubiera/hubiese puesto

Nos mudamos	*We move*
Querida, *vamos* a *poner* las plantas en tu auto, ¿no? Ya *he puesto* las maletas en el mío. Sí señor, *ponga* la mesa en el camión. Al llegar, *pondremos* todo en el comedor, ¿de acuerdo? ¿Dónde están las llaves de la casa? Creo que las *puse* en el auto. Miguel, *ponte* el abrigo, hace frío.	Darling, *we're going to put* the plants in your car, aren't we? *I've* already *put* the suitcases in mine. Yes, sir, *put* the table in the truck. When we arrive, *we'll put* everything in the dining room, OK? Where are the keys to the house? I think *I put* them in the car. Michael, *put* your coat on, it's cold.

(pg)

GERUND	PAST PARTICIPLE
queriendo	querido

PRESENT INDICATIVE	PRESENT PERFECT
quiero	he querido
quieres	
quiere	
queremos	
queréis	
quieren	

PRESENT PROGRESSIVE	IMPERFECT PROGRESSIVE
estoy queriendo	estaba queriendo

IMPERFECT INDICATIVE	PRETERITE
quería	quise
	quisiste
	quiso
	quisimos
	quisisteis
	quisieron

Note: This verb has the following irregularities:

- it is a stem-changing verb with **-e-** changing to **-ie-** when stressed;
- in addition, it has a **pretérito grave** with the stem **quis-**, also used in the imperfect subjunctive forms;
- the future and conditional stem is **querr-**.

IMPERATIVE
(tú) quiere   (vosotros) quered
(usted) quiera   (ustedes) quieran

PLUPERFECT   **PAST ANTERIOR**
había querido   hube querido

FUTURE   **FUTURE PERFECT**
querré   habré querido

CONDITIONAL   **CONDITIONAL PERFECT**
querría   habría/hubiera querido

PRESENT SUBJUNCTIVE   **PERFECT SUBJUNCTIVE**
quiera   haya querido
quieras
quiera
queramos
queráis
quieran

IMPERFECT SUBJUNCTIVE   **PLUPERFECT SUBJUNCTIVE**
quisiera/quisiese   hubiera/hubiese querido

Te *quiero* más de lo que *tú* me *quieres* a mi. | *I love* you more than *you love* me.

¡*Queremos* pan! | *We want* some bread!

Tienes que hacerlo, *quieras* o no. | You have to do it whether *you want to* or not.

Quisiéramos ir a Granada en primavera. | *We'd want to* go to Granada in the spring.

No sé si mi hermana *querrá* venir a la fiesta. | I don't know if my sister *will want to* come to the party.

Yo quería quedarme en casa, pero no pude. | I *wanted to* stay at home, but I couldn't.

GERUND	PAST PARTICIPLE
riendo	reído

PRESENT INDICATIVE	PRESENT PERFECT
río	he reído
ríes	
ríe	
reímos	
reís	
ríen	

PRESENT PROGRESSIVE	IMPERFECT PROGRESSIVE
estoy riendo	estaba riendo

IMPERFECT INDICATIVE	PRETERITE
reía	reí
	reiste
	rió
	reímos
	reísteis
	rieron

Similar verb

sonreír   smile

Note: This verb is actually a type 3 stem-changing verb like **pedir,** but any
form with a stressed **-i-** needs an accent.

IMPERATIVE
(tú) ríe   (vosotros) reíd
(usted) ría   (ustedes) rían

PLUPERFECT   **PAST ANTERIOR**
había reído   hube reído

FUTURE   **FUTURE PERFECT**
reiré   habré reído

CONDITIONAL   **CONDITIONAL PERFECT**
reiría   habría/hubiera reído

PRESENT SUBJUNCTIVE   **PERFECT SUBJUNCTIVE**
ría   haya reído
rías
ría
riamos
riais
rían

IMPERFECT SUBJUNCTIVE **PLUPERFECT SUBJUNCTIVE**
riera/riese   hubiera/hubiese reído

¡No *te rías* de mí!   Don't *laugh* at me!

¡No me hagas *reír*!   Don't make me *laugh*!

Ríete niño, no llores más.   *Laugh*, child, don't cry anymore.

La joven te *sonrió* antes de   The young woman *smiled* at you
salir.   before going out.

Reían como locos.   *They were laughing* like mad.

El público *se está riendo*   The audience *is laughing* very
mucho.   much.

50 romper(se)   break

GERUND	*PAST PARTICIPLE*
rompiendo	roto

PRESENT INDICATIVE	*PRESENT PERFECT*
rompo	he roto
rompes	
rompe	
rompemos	
rompéis	
rompen	

PRESENT PROGRESSIVE	*IMPERFECT PROGRESSIVE*
estoy rompiendo	estaba rompiendo

IMPERFECT INDICATIVE	*PRETERITE*
rompía	rompí
	rompiste
	rompió
	rompimos
	rompisteis
	rompieron

Note: This verb's only irregularity is its past participle, **roto**.

IMPERATIVE
(tú) rompe
(usted) rompa

(vosotros) romped
(ustedes) rompan

PLUPERFECT
había roto

PAST ANTERIOR
hube roto

FUTURE
romperé

FUTURE PERFECT
habré roto

CONDITIONAL
rompería

CONDITIONAL PERFECT
habría/hubiera roto

PRESENT SUBJUNCTIVE
rompa
rompas
rompa
rompamos
rompáis
rompan

PERFECT SUBJUNCTIVE
haya roto

IMPERFECT SUBJUNCTIVE
rompiera/rompiese

PLUPERFECT SUBJUNCTIVE
hubiera/hubiese roto

Mi amiga *se rompió* la pierna en el accidente.

My friend *broke* her leg in the accident.

¡No *me rompas* el cuaderno!

Don't break my notebook!

Todas las ventanas *estaban rotas*.

All of the windows *were broken*.

El borracho *está rompiendo* botellas en el bar.

The drunken man *is breaking* bottles in the bar.

51 saber   know; know how to; learn

(pg)

GERUND	PAST PARTICIPLE
sabiendo	sabido

PRESENT INDICATIVE	PRESENT PERFECT
sé	he sabido
sabes	
sabe	
sabemos	
sabéis	
saben	

PRESENT PROGRESSIVE	IMPERFECT PROGRESSIVE
estoy sabiendo	estaba sabiendo

IMPERFECT INDICATIVE	PRETERITE
sabía	supe
	supiste
	supo
	supimos
	supisteis
	supieron

Note: This verb has four irregularities:

- the first person singular form of the present indicative tense, **sé;**
- the whole of the present subjunctive tense, based on the stem **sep-;**
- the **pretérito grave** with the stem **sup-,** also used for the imperfect subjunctive forms;
- the future tense stem **sabr-,** also used in the conditional forms.

Note that in its preterite forms, this verb means *to learn.*

IMPERATIVE
(tú) sabe   (vosotros) sabed
(usted) sepa   (ustedes) sepan

PLUPERFECT	*PAST ANTERIOR*
había sabido	hube sabido

FUTURE	*FUTURE PERFECT*
sabré	habré sabido

CONDITIONAL	*CONDITIONAL PERFECT*
sabría	habría/hubiera sabido

PRESENT SUBJUNCTIVE	*PERFECT SUBJUNCTIVE*
sepa	haya sabido
sepas	
sepa	
sepamos	
sepáis	
sepan	

IMPERFECT SUBJUNCTIVE	*PLUPERFECT SUBJUNCTIVE*
supiera/supiese	hubiera/hubiese sabido

¡No *sabes* nada!	*You don't know anything!*
Que *yo sepa*, el niño tendría unos diez años.	As far as *I know*, the child would be about ten years old.
Sabes esquiar, ¿verdad?	*You do know how to ski*, don't you?
Al llegar a casa, *supe* que mi tía había muerto.	When I got home, *I learned* that my aunt had died.
Sí, sí, ya lo *sé*.	Yes, yes, *I know* it.

GERUND	PAST PARTICIPLE
saliendo	salido

PRESENT INDICATIVE	PRESENT PERFECT
salgo	he salido
sales	
sale	
salimos	
salís	
salen	

PRESENT PROGRESSIVE	IMPERFECT PROGRESSIVE
estoy saliendo	estaba saliendo

IMPERFECT INDICATIVE	PRETERITE
salía	salí
	saliste
	salió
	salimos
	salisteis
	salieron

Note: This verb has three irregularities:

• the first person singular form of the present indicative tense, and so all forms of the present subjunctive tense, which have the stem **salg-**;
• the singular informal imperative is **sal**;
• the irregular stem **saldr-,** used for the future and conditional tenses.

IMPERATIVE
(tú) sal   (vosotros) salid
(usted) salga   (ustedes) salgan

PLUPERFECT   *PAST ANTERIOR*
había salido   hube salido

FUTURE   *FUTURE PERFECT*
saldré   habré salido

CONDITIONAL   *CONDITIONAL PERFECT*
saldría   habría / hubiera salido

PRESENT SUBJUNCTIVE   *PERFECT SUBJUNCTIVE*
salga   haya salido
salgas
salga
salgamos
salgáis
salgan

IMPERFECT SUBJUNCTIVE   *PLUPERFECT SUBJUNCTIVE*
saliera / saliese   hubiera / hubiese salido

¡*Sal* de ahí!   *Get out* of there!

No *salgo* mucho, pues no tengo   I *don't go out* much, because
tiempo, pero *saldremos* mañana   I don't have time, but *we'll go out*
si quieres.   tomorrow if you want.

Salgan con cuidado, por favor.   *Get out* carefully, please.

Espero que todo *salga* bien.   I hope everything *comes out* well.

GERUND	*PAST PARTICIPLE*
siendo	sido

PRESENT INDICATIVE	*PRESENT PERFECT*
soy	he sido
eres	
es	
somos	
sois	
son	

PRESENT PROGRESSIVE	*IMPERFECT PROGRESSIVE*
estoy siendo	estaba siendo

IMPERFECT INDICATIVE	*PRETERITE*
era	fui
eras	fuiste
era	fue
éramos	fuimos
erais	fuisteis
eran	fueron

Note: This highly irregular verb should be learned thoroughly, noting the following features:

- the first person singular form of the present indicative tense is **soy,** and the rest of the forms of this tense are highly irregular, as it happens with the imperative forms;
- the present subjunctive tense is based on the form **sea;**
- the preterite tense is highly irregular, and its stem is used for the imperfect subjunctive tense (in both of these, **ser** shares its forms with **ir**);
- the imperfect tense is based on the form **era;**
- other tenses are apparently regular: the gerund, the past participle, the future, and the conditional.

Note also that **ser** is used to form the passive, together with the past participle of the main verb [➤The Verb System in Spanish].

IMPERATIVE
(tú) sé   (vosotros) sed
(usted) sea   (ustedes) sean

PLUPERFECT   *PAST ANTERIOR*
había sido   hube sido

FUTURE   *FUTURE PERFECT*
seré   habré sido

CONDITIONAL   *CONDITIONAL PERFECT*
sería   habría/hubiera sido

PRESENT SUBJUNCTIVE   *PERFECT SUBJUNCTIVE*
sea   haya sido
seas
sea
seamos
seáis
sean

IMPERFECT SUBJUNCTIVE   *PLUPERFECT SUBJUNCTIVE*
fuera/fuese   hubiera/hubiese sido

¡**Sé** bueno, o me enfadaré contigo!

Be good or I'll get angry at you!

Hemos sido amigos desde hace años.

We've been friends for years.

Eran las dos de la tarde.

It was two in the afternoon.

Soy soltero, ¡pero espero que no lo **sea** para siempre!

I'm a bachelor, but I hope *I won't* always *be* one!

Fueron cinco niños los que ganaron el concurso.

There were five children who won the contest.

Si **yo fuera** más joven, dormiría menos.

If *I were* younger, I would sleep less.

(pg)

GERUND	PAST PARTICIPLE
teniendo	tenido

PRESENT INDICATIVE	PRESENT PERFECT
tengo	he tenido
tienes	
tiene	
tenemos	
tenéis	
tienen	

PRESENT PROGRESSIVE	IMPERFECT PROGRESSIVE
estoy teniendo	estaba teniendo

IMPERFECT INDICATIVE	PRETERITE
tenía	tuve
	tuviste
	tuvo
	tuvimos
	tuvisteis
	tuvieron

Similar verbs

abstenerse	abstain	**entretener**	entertain
contener	contain, hold	**mantener**	maintain, provide
detener	stop, detain, arrest		for, support
sostener	hold up, support, sustain	**obtener**	get, obtain

Note: The main irregular features of this verb are:

• the first person singular form of the present tense is **tengo**, and so the present subjunctive forms have the stem **teng-**;
• the rest of the present indicative forms behave like an **e** → **ie** stem-changing verb;
• the **pretérito grave** stem is **tuv-**, also used for the imperfect subjunctive forms;
• the future and conditional stem is **tendr-**;
• the singular informal imperative is **ten**.

IMPERATIVE

(tú) ten	(vosotros) tened
(usted) tenga	(ustedes) tengan

PLUPERFECT	**PAST ANTERIOR**
había tenido	hube tenido
FUTURE	**FUTURE PERFECT**
tendré	habré tenido
CONDITIONAL	**CONDITIONAL PERFECT**
tendría	habría/hubiera tenido
PRESENT SUBJUNCTIVE	**PERFECT SUBJUNCTIVE**
tenga	haya tenido
tengas	
tenga	
tengamos	
tongáis	
tengan	
IMPERFECT SUBJUNCTIVE	**PLUPERFECT SUBJUNCTIVE**
tuviera/tuviese	hubiera/hubiese tenido

Tenemos prisa.	*We're in* a hurry.
Tenga piedad de nosotros.	*Have* mercy on us.
Ha tenido mucho que hacer.	*She has had* a lot to do.
Teníamos mucho dinero.	*We had* a lot of money.
Tuvieron que salir.	*They had to* go out.
Si tuviera dinero lo compraría.	If *I had* money, I would buy it.
Tendremos que trabajar todo el fin de semana.	*We will have to* work all weekend.

(pg)

GERUND	PAST PARTICIPLE
trayendo	traído

PRESENT INDICATIVE	PRESENT PERFECT
traigo	he traído
traes	
trae	
traemos	
traéis	
traen	

PRESENT PROGRESSIVE	IMPERFECT PROGRESSIVE
estoy trayendo	estaba trayendo

INDICATIVE IMPERFECT	PRETERITE
traía	traje
	trajiste
	trajo
	trajimos
	trajisteis
	trajeron

Similar verbs

atraer	attract, lure	**distraer**	distract
contraer	contract	**sustraer**	subtract

Note: The irregular features of this verb are:

- the first person singular form of the present indicative tense is **traigo,** making the present subjunctive stem **traig-;**
- the **pretérito grave** stem is **traj-,** used also for the imperfect subjunctive forms; note the missing **-i-** of the third person plural form;
- any form with an ending beginning with **-i-** has a **-y-** instead (except for the third person plural form of the preterite tense as explained above);
- the **-i-** of the past participle needs an accent.

IMPERATIVE	
(tú) trae	(vosotros) traed
(usted) traiga	(ustedes) traigan

PLUPERFECT	PAST ANTERIOR
había traído	hube traído

FUTURE	FUTURE PERFECT
traeré	habré traído

CONDITIONAL	CONDITIONAL PERFECT
traería	habría/hubiera traido

PRESENT SUBJUNCTIVE

PERFECT SUBJUNCTIVE

PRESENT SUBJUNCTIVE	PERFECT SUBJUNCTIVE
traiga	haya traído
traigas	
traiga	
traigamos	
traigáls	
traigan	

IMPERFECT SUBJUNCTIVE	PLUPERFECT SUBJUNCTIVE
trajera/trajese	hubiera/hubiese traído

Tráigame más pan, por favor.	*Bring me* more bread, please.
Traje sólo dos mil pesetas.	*I* only *brought* two thousand pesetas.
Mi esposa siempre me traía un recuerdo de sus viajes.	My wife always *brought* me a souvenir from her trips.
¿Traerás tú la comida?	*Will you bring* the food?

GERUND	PAST PARTICIPLE
valiendo	valido

PRESENT INDICATIVE	PRESENT PERFECT
valgo	he valido
vales	
vale	
valemos	
valéis	
valen	

PRESENT PROGRESSIVE	IMPERFECT PROGRESSIVE
estoy valiendo	estaba valiendo

IMPERFECT INDICATIVE	PRETERITE
valía	valí
	valiste
	valió
	valimos
	valisteis
	valieron

Note: The only irregular features of this verb are:

• the first person singular form of the present indicative tense is **valgo,** making the present subjunctive stem **valg-;**
• the stem of the future and conditional tenses is **valdr-**

IMPERATIVE
(tú) vale
(usted) valga

(vosotros) valed
(ustedes) valgan

PLUPERFECT
había valido

PAST ANTERIOR
hube valido

FUTURE
valdré

FUTURE PERFECT
habré valido

CONDITIONAL
valdría

CONDITIONAL PERFECT
habría/hubiera valido

PRESENT SUBJUNCTIVE
valga
valgas
valga
valgamos
valgáis
valgan

PERFECT SUBJUNCTIVE
haya valido

IMPERFECT SUBJUNCTIVE
valiera/valiese

PLUPERFECT SUBJUNCTIVE
hubiera/hubiese valido

No *vale* la pena volver.

It's not *worth* coming back.

Estas camisas *valían* sólo cinco pesos.

These shirts *cost* only five pesos.

Si esa pintura *valiera* tanto como sugieres, no la estarían regalando.

If that painting *were worth* as much as you suggest, they wouldn't be giving it away.

(pg)

GERUND	PAST PARTICIPLE
viniendo	venido

PRESENT INDICATIVE	PRESENT PERFECT
vengo	he venido
vienes	
viene	
venimos	
venís	
vienen	

PRESENT PROGRESSIVE	IMPERFECT PROGRESSIVE
estoy viniendo	estaba viniendo

IMPERFECT INDICATIVE	PRETERITE
venía	vine
	viniste
	vino
	vinimos
	vinisteis
	vinieron

Similar verbs

contravenir	contravene	**intervenir**	intervene
convenir	fit, suit		

Note: The main irregular features of this verb are:

- the first person singular form of the present indicative tense is **vengo,** so the present subjunctive forms have the stem **veng-;**
- the rest of the present indicative forms behave like an **e** → **ie** stem-changing verb;
- the **pretérito grave** stem is **vin-,** also used for the imperfect subjunctive tense and the gerund,
- the future and conditional stem is **vendr-;**
- the singular informal imperative is **ven.**

IMPERATIVE
(tú) ven
(usted) venga

(vosotros) venid
(ustedes) vengan

PLUPERFECT
había venido

PAST INTERIOR
hube venido

FUTURE
vendré

FUTURE PERFECT
habré venido

CONDITIONAL
vendría

CONDITIONAL PERFECT
habría/hubiera venido

PRESENT SUBJUNCTIVE
venga
vengas
venga
vengamos
vengáis
vengan

PERFECT SUBJUNCTIVE
haya venido

IMPERFECT SUBJUNCTIVE
viniera/viniese

PLUPERFECT SUBJUNCTIVE
hubiera/hubiese venido

Venga conmigo a la comisaría.
Come with me to the police station.

Vinieron en el tren de las doce.
They came on the twelve o'clock train.

Venía a tiempo todos los días.
He came on time every day.

Vendremos a verte mañana.
We'll come to see you tomorrow.

GERUND	PAST PARTICIPLE
viendo	visto

PRESENT INDICATIVE	PRESENT PERFECT
veo	he visto
ves	
ve	
vemos	
veis	
ven	

PRESENT PROGRESSIVE	IMPERFECT PROGRESSIVE
estoy viendo	estaba viendo

IMPERFECT INDICATIVE	PRETERITE
veía	vi
	viste
	vio
	vimos
	visteis
	vieron

Similar verbs

entrever   glimpse   **prever**   foresee, forecast

Note: The main irregular features of this verb are:

> • the stem of the first person singular form of the present indicative
> tense, all of the present subjunctive forms, and the imperfect indica-
> tive tense is **ve-;**
> • the preterite forms are the same as for **-er** and **-ir** verbs, but with no
> written accents;
> • the past participle is irregular: **visto.**

> In other respects, **ver** is regular, but note that the singular informal
> imperative—**ve**—is identical to that of **ir.**

IMPERATIVE	
(tú) ve	(vosotros) ved
(usted) vea	(ustedes) vean

PLUPERFECT	*PAST ANTERIOR*
había visto	hube visto

FUTURE	*FUTURE PERFECT*
veré	habré visto

CONDITIONAL	*CONDITIONAL PERFECT*
vería	habría/hubiera visto

PRESENT SUBJUNCTIVE	*PERFECT SUBJUNCTIVE*
vea	haya visto
veas	
vea	
veamos	
veáis	
vean	

IMPERFECT SUBJUNCTIVE	*PLUPERFECT SUBJUNCTIVE*
viera/viese	hubiera/hubiese visto

¡Te *veo* claramente!	*I see* you clearly!
Nos *vieron* entrar en el café.	*They saw* us going into the café.
Había visto a su madre llorando.	*He had seen* his mother crying.
Estamos viendo una película muy buena en la televisión.	*We are watching* a very good movie on television.
Los economistas *prevén* que la inflación aumentará.	The economists *foresee* that inflation will go up.

C
SUBJECT INDEX

SUBJECT INDEX

The numbers given below refer to the relevant section in The Verb System in Spanish.

D
VERB INDEX

An asterisk next to a verb indicates that it is one of the Model Verbs listed in section B.

Whenever the letters **ch**, **ll**, and **ñ** appear, English alphabetical order has been used throughout.

A

abandonar *(tr)*	abandon, desert, leave behind **2**
abastecer *(tr)*	provide, supply **32**
ablandar *(tr)*	soften **2**
abolir *(tr)*	abolish **4**
abordar *(tr)*	approach, board **2**
aborrecer *(tr)*	hate, abhor **32**
abortar *(intr)*	abort, miscarry **2**
abotonar *(tr)*	button **2**
abrasar *(tr)*	scorch **2**
abrazar(se) *(tr/refl)*	embrace, hug **6**
abrevar *(tr)*	water (*animals*) **2**
abreviar(se) *(tr/refl)*	shorten, become shorter **14**
abrigar(se) *(tr/refl)*	shelter **7**
***abrir** *(tr/intr)*	open; open up **25**
abrir *(tr)*	turn on (*faucet/tap*)
abrir con llave *(tr)*	unlock
abrir por la fuerza *(tr)*	force one's way into
abrochar *(tr)*	button, fasten **2**
absolver *(tr)*	absolve, let off **20**
absorber *(tr)*	absorb **3**
abstenerse de *(refl)*	abstain from, refrain from **54**
abultar *(tr)*	increase, enlarge **2**
abundar *(intr)*	abound, be abundant **2**
aburrir *(tr)*	bore **4**
abusar de *(tr)*	misuse, abuse **2**
acabar *(tr)*	finish, complete **2**
acabar con *(tr)*	finish with; do away with
acabar de	have just
acabar(se) *(intr/refl)*	end, finish; end up **2**
acallar *(tr)*	silence **2**
acampar(se) *(intr/refl)*	camp **2**
acanalar *(tr)*	channel **2**
acariciar *(tr)*	caress, pet, fondle, cherish **2**

acarrear *(tr)*	haul **2**
acechar *(tr)*	lie in wait for **2**
acelerar *(tr)*	accelerate, speed up **2**
aceptar *(tr)*	accept **2**
acerar *(tr)*	steel **2**
acercar *(tr)*	bring near **5**
acercarse a *(refl)*	approach **5**
acertar *(tr/intr)*	hit the mark **19**
aclarar *(tr)*	clarify, clear up; rinse **2**
acoger *(tr)*	welcome **11**
acometer *(tr)*	attack; undertake **3**
acomodar *(tr)*	accommodate, lodge, put up; suit **2**
acompañar *(tr)*	accompany **2**
aconsejar *(tr)*	advise **2**
acontecer *(intr)*	happen, occur **32**
acoplar(se) *(tr/refl)*	mate **2**
acordar *(tr)*	tune **20**
acordarse de *(refl)*	remember **20**
acortar(se) *(tr/refl)*	draw in, shorten, become shorter **2**
acosar *(tr)*	harass, hound, pester **2**
acostar *(tr)*	put to bed **20**
acostarse *(refl)*	go to bed, lie (down) **20**
acostumbrar *(tr)*	accustom **2**
acostumbrarse a *(refl)*	become accustomed, get used to **2**
acribillar *(tr)*	riddle; pester **2**
actualizar *(tr)*	modernize, update **6**
***actuar** *(tr/intr)*	act, do, perform **15**
actuar de mimo *(intr)*	mime
acudir *(intr)*	gather around; show up, turn up **4**
acumular(se) *(tr/refl)*	accumulate, collect, mount up **2**
acunar *(tr)*	rock (to sleep) **2**
acuñar *(tr)*	strike (*coin, medal*); wedge **2**
acusar *(tr)*	accuse, charge **2**
adaptar *(tr)*	adapt; suit **2**
adaptarse a *(refl)*	adapt, adjust to **2**

adelantar *(tr/intr)*	advance, move forward, overtake **2**
adelgazar *(tr/intr)*	get thin, lose weight, reduce, slim, thin down **6**
adherirse a *(refl)*	adhere to, cling to, stick **4**
adiestrar *(tr)*	train; drill **2**
adivinar *(tr/intr)*	guess **2**
administrar *(tr)*	administer **2**
administrar una dosis *(tr)*	administer a dose
admirar *(tr)*	admire **2**
admirarse *(refl)*	wonder **2**
admitir *(intr)*	accept, acknowledge, admit **4**
adoptar *(tr)*	adopt **2**
adorar *(tr)*	adore, worship **2**
adornar *(tr)*	adorn, decorate, embellish **2**
***adquirir** *(tr)*	acquire; get; purchase **26**
aducir *(tr)*	adduce **31**
adular *(tr)*	flatter **2**
advertir *(tr)*	warn **22**
afanarse *(refl)*	slog away, work hard **2**
afectar *(tr)*	affect **2**
afeitar(se) *(tr/refl)*	shave **2**
aferrarse a *(refl)*	stick to, cling to **2**
aficionarse a *(refl)*	take to **2**
afilar *(tr)*	sharpen; taper **2**
afinar *(tr)*	refine; tune **2**
afirmar *(tr)*	affirm, declare, say, state **2**
afligir *(tr)*	afflict, sadden, trouble **11**
aflojar(se) *(tr/refl)*	loosen, slacken **2**
agacharse *(refl)*	crouch, squat **2**
agarrar *(tr)*	grab, grasp, grip, hold, seize, snatch **2**
agarrarse de *(refl)*	hold on, grab hold of **2**
agitar *(tr)*	stir; wag, wave **2**
agitarse *(refl)*	tremble **2**
agonizar *(intr)*	agonize **6**
agotar *(tr)*	exhaust, drain **2**
agradar *(tr)*	please **2**
agradecer *(tr)*	thank **32**

agravar(se) *(tr/refl)*	worsen **2**
agraviar *(tr)*	wrong **2**
agregar *(tr)*	add **7**
agriar(se) *(tr/refl)*	sour **14**
aguantar *(tr/intr)*	bear, endure, hold out, put up with **2**
aguar *(tr)*	water/thin down (*wine*, etc.) **8**
aguardar *(tr)*	wait **2**
agujerear *(tr)*	pierce, make a hole in **2**
ahogar(se) *(tr/refl)*	drown; suffocate **7**
ahorrar *(tr)*	put away, save (*money, time*) **2**
ahuecar *(tr)*	hollow out **5**
ahusarse *(refl)*	taper **2**
aislar *(tr)*	isolate **15**
ajustar *(tr)*	adjust, regulate; settle (*accounts*); suit **2**
alabar *(tr)*	praise **2**
alargar(se) *(tr/refl)*	extend, lengthen, stretch **7**
alarmar *(tr)*	alarm, frighten **2**
alborear *(intr)*	dawn **2**
alborotar *(intr)*	make a racket, brawl **2**
alcanzar *(tr/intr)*	reach, get to, attain **6**
alejar *(tr)*	alienate, distance, move away **2**
alejarse *(refl)*	go away **2**
alentar *(tr)*	encourage; breathe **2**
aligerar *(tr)*	lighten **2**
alimentar *(tr)*	feed **2**
alinear(se) *(tr/refl)*	align, line up **2**
alisar *(tr)*	flatten, smooth **2**
alistarse *(refl)*	get ready; join up (*armed services*) **2**
aliviar *(tr)*	alleviate, deaden (*pain*), relieve **2**
allanar *(tr)*	flatten, level, smooth **2**
almacenar *(tr)*	hoard, store **2**
almorzar *(intr)*	have lunch **6, 20**
alojar *(tr)*	accommodate, house, lodge, put up **2**

VERB INDEX

alquilar *(tr)*	charter, let, rent, rent out	**2**
alterar *(tr)*	upset, disturb	**2**
alternar *(intr)*	alternate	**2**
aludir a *(intr)*	refer to	**4**
alumbrar *(tr)*	light (up)	**2**
alzar *(tr)*	hoist, lift, raise	**6**
amalgamar *(tr)*	amalgamate	**2**
amamantar *(tr)*	suckle	**2**
amanecer *(intr)*	dawn	**32**
amansar *(tr)*	tame	**2**
***amar** *(tr)*	love	**1**
amargar *(tr)*	sour	**7**
amarrar *(tr)*	fasten, moor, tie up	**2**
amarrar con una cuerda *(tr)*	rope together	
amenazar *(tr)*	threaten	**6**
amoldar *(tr)*	mold	**2**
amontonar *(tr)*	heap, hoard	**2**
amontonar(se) *(tr/refl)*	huddle, pile	**2**
amortiguar *(tr)*	deaden, muffle	**8**
amortizar *(tr)*	pay off	**6**
amotinarse *(refl)*	riot	**2**
ampliar *(tr)*	enlarge, expand, widen	**14**
amplificar *(tr)*	amplify	**5**
ampollar(se) *(tr/refl)*	blister	**2**
amputar *(tr)*	amputate	**2**
analizar *(tr)*	analyze	**6**
anclar *(intr)*	anchor	**2**
***andar** *(intr)*	walk, go around; function, work	**27**
andar a gatas *(intr)*	crawl, creep	
andar a pasos largos *(intr)*	stride	
andar con paso majestuoso *(intr)*	sweep (*movement*)	
aneblarse *(refl)*	become misty	**2**
anestesiar *(tr)*	anesthetize	**2**
anexar *(tr)*	annex	**2**
anhelar *(tr)*	long for	**2**
anidar *(tr/intr)*	nest	**2**
animar *(tr)*	animate, encourage	**2**

animarse *(refl)*	brighten up, cheer up; bear up **2**
aniquilar *(tr)*	annihilate **2**
anochecer *(intr)*	get dark **32**
anotar *(tr)*	write down **2**
anticipar *(tr)*	anticipate; advance (*payment*) **2**
anudar *(tr)*	knot **2**
anular *(tr)*	annul, cancel out, write off (*insurance, debt*) **2**
anunciar *(tr)*	advertise, announce **2**
añadir *(tr)*	add **4**
apacentar *(tr)*	graze **2**
apaciguar *(tr)*	appease, pacify **8**
apagar *(tr)*	extinguish, put out; quench; switch off, turn off **7**
apagarse *(refl)*	go out, die away **7**
aparcar *(tr)*	park **5**
aparecer *(intr)*	appear **32**
aparecer inesperadamente *(intr)*	pop up
aparentar *(tr)*	pretend **2**
apartar *(tr)*	move away; separate **2**
apartarse de *(refl)*	diverge from **2**
apedrear *(tr)*	stone **2**
apelar *(tr/intr)*	appeal **2**
apercibir *(tr)*	catch sight of **4**
apetecer *(tr)*	feel like, want **32**
apilar(se) *(tr/refl)*	pile **3**
aplastar *(tr)*	crush **2**
aplaudir *(tr/intr)*	applaud, clap **4**
aplazar *(tr)*	adjourn, defer, postpone, procrastinate **6**
aplicar *(tr)*	apply **5**
aporrear *(tr)*	bash, beat up **2**
apostar *(tr/intr)*	bet, stake **20**
apoyar *(tr)*	hold up, side with, support, back, back (up); prop, shore up; stand by, uphold **2**

VERB INDEX

apoyar(se) *(tr/refl)*	lean **2**
apreciar *(tr)*	appreciate, cherish; assess, prize, value **2**
aprender *(tr)*	learn **3**
aprender de memoria *(tr)*	learn by heart
apresurarse *(refl)*	hurry, make haste, speed **2**
apretar(se) *(tr/refl)*	press (*button*, etc.); tighten (*nut*); squeeze **19**
aprisionar *(tr)*	imprison, trap **2**
aprobar *(tr/intr)*	approve, agree to; pass (*exam, law*) **20**
aprovechar(se) de *(tr)*	to take advantage of **2**
aproximarse *(refl)*	approximate **2**
apuntar *(tr)*	note down, note, record, write down **2**
apuntar a *(tr)*	aim
apuñalar *(tr)*	stab **2**
arañar *(tr)*	scratch **2**
arar *(tr)*	plow **2**
arbitrar *(tr)*	referee **2**
arbitrar entre *(intr)*	arbitrate between
archivar *(tr)*	file **2**
arder *(intr)*	blaze burn **3**
arder de *(tr)*	inflame with
armar *(tr)*	arm **2**
armonizar *(tr)*	harmonize **6**
arrancar *(intr)*	boot up (*computing*); start, start up **5**
arrastrar *(tr)*	drag, haul, heave, trail **2**
arrastrarse *(refl)*	crawl, creep, drag **2**
arrebatar *(tr)*	snatch **2**
arreglar *(tr)*	arrange, fix, settle; sort out, mend, repair; tidy up, trim **2**
arreglárselas *(refl)*	cope **2**
arrendar *(tr)*	lease (out), rent, rent out **19**
arrepentirse *(refl)*	regret, repent **22**
arrestar *(tr)*	arrest **2**
arriesgar *(tr)*	chance, risk **7**
arriesgarse *(refl)*	dare, venture, risk **7**

arrodillarse *(refl)*	kneel (down) **2**
arrojar *(tr)*	cast, fling, hurl, pitch, throw **2**
arrollar *(tr/intr)*	coil, roll up **2**
arrugar(se) *(tr/refl)*	wrinkle, ruffle **7**
arruinar *(tr)*	bankrupt, make a mess of, ruin, wreck **2**
asaltar *(tr)*	assault, storm **2**
asar *(tr)*	roast **2**
asar a la parrilla *(tr)*	grill
ascender *(tr)*	advance (*rank*), promote **19**
ascender *(intr)*	ascend, go up **19**
ascender a *(intr)*	add up to, amount to, number
asediar *(tr)*	besiege **2**
asegurar *(tr)*	assure, ensure, make safe, secure, underwrite **2**
asegurar(se) *(tr/refl)*	insure **2**
asentir *(intr)*	agree, assent **19**
asesinar *(tr)*	assassinate, murder, slaughter **2**
asfixiar(se) *(tr/refl)*	suffocate, throttle **2**
asignar *(tr)*	allocate, assign **2**
asimilar *(tr)*	assimilate **2**
***asir(se)** *(tr)*	seize; grasp; grab; snatch **18**
asistir *(tr)*	assist **4**
asistir a *(tr/intr)*	witness; be present at **4**
asociarse *(refl)*	associate, band together **2**
asociarse con *(refl)*	team up with
asolar *(tr)*	devastate **2**
asomar(se) *(tr/refl)*	lean out, stick out **2**
asombrar *(tr)*	amaze, surprise **2**
asombrarse *(refl)*	wonder **2**
aspirar *(intr)*	inhale **2**
aspirar a *(intr)*	aim, aspire **2**
astillar *(tr)*	chip, splinter **2**
asumir *(tr)*	assume **4**
asustar *(tr)*	frighten, scare **2**
asustarse *(refl)*	get scared **2**
atacar *(tr)*	attack **5**
atajar *(tr/intr)*	cut across, intercept **2**

atar *(tr)*	tie, tie up **2**
atar con una cuerda *(tr)*	rope together
atender *(tr)*	assist; care for, nurse, tend, treat (*medically*) **19**
atenerse a *(refl)*	abide by, hold to **54**
aterrar *(tr)*	terrify **2**
aterrizar *(intr)*	land **6**
aterrorizar *(tr)*	terrify, terrorize **6**
atiborrarse de comida *(refl)*	stuff oneself with food **2**
atiesar(se) *(tr/refl)*	harden, stiffen, tighten **2**
atomizar *(tr)*	atomize **6**
atormentar *(tr)*	torment **2**
atornillar *(tr)*	screw **2**
atracar *(tr/intr)*	moor, tie up (*nautical*) **5**
atraer *(tr)*	attract, lure **55**
atragantarse *(refl)*	choke **2**
atrancar *(tr)*	bar, bolt (*door*) **5**
atrapar *(tr)*	trap **2**
atravesar *(tr/intr)*	cross, go across; shoot (*rapids*) **19**
atreverse *(refl)*	dare **3**
atropellar *(tr)*	knock over, run down, run over **2**
auditar *(tr)*	audit **2**
aullar *(intr)*	howl **2**
aumentar *(tr/ntr)*	add to, increase, raise, rise **2**
ausentarse *(refl)*	absent oneself, play truant **2**
automatizar *(tr)*	automate **2**
autorizar *(tr)*	authorize, entitle **2**
avanzar *(tr/intr)*	advance, move forward **6**
aventajar *(tr)*	surpass, top **2**
aventurar *(tr)*	gamble, venture **2**
avergonzar(se) *(tr/refl)*	shame; be ashamed **6**
averiarse *(refl)*	get damaged; break down **14**
***averiguar** *(tr)*	verify; find out; look up; know **8**
avisar *(tr)*	inform, warn **2**
avistar *(tr)*	sight **2**
ayudar *(tr)*	aid, help **2**
ayunar *(intr)*	fast **2**

azorar *(tr)*	disturb, embarrass, upset **2**
azotar *(tr)*	whip **2**
azucarar *(tr)*	sugar, sweeten **2**

B

babear *(intr)*	dribble **2**
bailar *(intr)*	dance **2**
bajar *(tr)*	let down, lower, pull down, take down **2**
bajar *(intr)*	come down, go down, get down, descend; decline, lessen; ebb *(tide)*, subside *(water)* **2**
bajar de *(intr)*	alight, get off, get out of
balancear(se) *(tr/refl)*	rock, sway, swing **2**
balar *(intr)*	bleat **2**
balbucear *(tr/intr)*	stammer, stutter **2**
bambolearse *(intr)*	sway, totter **2**
banquetear *(tr/intr)*	feast **2**
bañar *(tr)*	bath, bathe, dip **2**
bañarse *(refl)*	take a bath **2**
barrear *(tr)*	barricade **2**
barrer *(tr)*	sweep **3**
basar en *(tr)*	base on **2**
bastar *(intr)*	be enough, do, suffice **2**
batir *(tr)*	beat; hammer **4**
bautizar *(tr)*	baptize **6**
beber *(tr)*	drink **3**
*bendecir *(tr)*	bless **28**
beneficiar *(tr)*	benefit, do good to **2**
besar *(tr)*	kiss **2**
bifurcarse *(intr)*	fork **5**
blandir *(tr)*	brandish, flourish **4**
blanquear(se) *(tr/refl)*	bleach, whiten **2**
blasfemar *(intr)*	blaspheme, curse **2**
bloquear *(tr)*	block, stop, trap **2**
boicotear *(tr)*	boycott **2**
bombardear *(tr)*	bomb, bombard, shell **2**
bombear *(tr)*	pump **2**

bombearse *(refl)*	bulge, warp **2**
borbotar *(intr)*	boil over, bubble **2**
bordar *(tr)*	embroider **2**
borrar *(tr)*	delete, erase, rub out, scrub, wipe out **2**
bostezar *(intr)*	yawn **6**
boxear *(intr)*	box **2**
bramar *(intr)*	bellow, roar **2**
brasear *(tr)*	braise **2**
brillar *(tr/intr)*	gleam, glow, shine **2**
brincar *(intr)*	hop, skip **5**
brindar *(tr)*	toast (*with drink*) **2**
bromear *(intr)*	joke **2**
broncear(se) *(tr/refl)*	tan **2**
brotar *(intr)*	spring (from), sprout (from), well up **2**
burbujear *(intr)*	bubble **2**
burlar *(tr)*	circumvent, deceive **2**
buscar *(tr)*	look for, look up, search, seek **5**

C

cabalgar *(tr/intr)*	ride (*horse*) **7**
cabecear *(intr)*	nod (*sleepily*), shake one's head **2**
***caber** *(intr)*	fit **29**
caducar *(tr)*	fall due; expire **5**
***caer(se)** *(intr)*	fall, drop **30**
caer enfermo *(intr)*	fall ill
calar *(tr)*	go through, penetrate **2**
calar(se) *(tr/refl)*	drench, soak **2**
calcular *(tr)*	calculate, compute **2**
calentar(se) *(tr/refl)*	heat, warm, warm up **19**
calificar *(tr)*	define, call, describe, qualify **5**
callarse *(refl)*	shut up
calmar(se) *(tr/refl)*	calm (down), cool (down) **2**
calumniar *(tr)*	slander **2**
calzar *(tr)*	put shoes on, shoe **6**
cambiar *(tr/intr)*	change, exchange, switch, vary; shift (e.g., *weather*) **2**

cambiar por *(tr)*	trade, exchange
cambiarse *(refl)*	change into, turn **2**
caminar *(intr)*	step, walk **2**
cancelar *(tr)*	call off, cancel, write off (*insurance, debt*) **2**
cansar(se) *(tr/refl)*	tire **2**
cantar *(tr/intr)*	sing **2**
canturrear *(intr)*	hum (*person*) **2**
capturar *(tr)*	capture **2**
caracterizar *(tr)*	characterize **6**
carecer *(intr)*	lack **32**
cargar *(tr)*	charge, load; debit (*account*) **7**
caricaturizar *(tr)*	caricature **6**
casar(se) *(tr/refl)*	get married, marry **2**
castigar *(tr)*	punish **7**
catalogar *(tr)*	catalogue, list **7**
causar *(tr)*	cause **2**
cavar *(tr/intr)*	dig **2**
***cazar** *(tr/intr)*	hunt, chase **6**
cazar ilegalmente *(tr)*	poach
cebar *(tr)*	fatten, feed **2**
cebar *(intr)*	grip, catch (*nut*) **2**
ceder *(tr/intr)*	cede, compromise, give in, give up, yield **3**
ceder el paso *(intr)*	give way
cegar *(tr)*	blind **7, 19**
celebrar *(tr)*	celebrate **2**
cenar *(tr/intr)*	dine, have supper **2**
censurar *(tr)*	censor, censure **2**
centellear *(intr)*	sparkle **2**
centralizar *(tr)*	centralize **6**
centrifugar *(tr)*	spin **7**
ceñir *(tr)*	skirt, surround **17**
cepillar *(tr)*	brush **2**
cercar *(tr)*	circle, close in, enclose, fence (in), surround **5**
cercar con un seto *(tr)*	hedge
cerrar(se) *(tr/refl)*	close, shut; turn off (*faucet*) **19**
cerrar con llave *(tr)*	lock

cerrar la cremallera *(tr)*	zip up
cerrar(se) de golpe *(tr/refl)*	slam
certificar *(tr)*	certify **5**
cesar *(intr)*	stop **2**
chantajear *(tr)*	blackmail **2**
chapotear *(intr)*	splash about **2**
charlar *(intr)*	chat, talk **2**
chasquear *(intr)*	crack, creak (*wood*) **2**
chillar *(intr)*	howl, scream, squeal **2**
chirriar *(intr)*	creak, squeal **2**
chispear *(intr)*	sparkle **2**
chocar *(tr)*	shock **5**
chocar con *(tr)*	crash into, hit, run into
chocar contra *(tr)*	bump into, knock against, smash into
chupar *(tr)*	suck **2**
chutar *(tr)*	shoot (*soccer*) **2**
circular *(tr)*	circulate **2**
citar *(tr)*	quote; date **2**
citarse con *(refl)*	make an appointment with **2**
clasificar(se) *(tr/refl)*	classify, file, grade **5**
clausurar *(tr)*	close down **2**
clavar *(tr)*	drive in (*nail*), nail, nail down **2**
cobrar *(tr)*	cash; charge (*price*) **2**
cocer *(tr)*	cook **9, 20**
cocer a fuego lento *(tr/intr)*	simmer
cocer al vapor *(tr)*	steam
cocinar *(tr)*	cook **2**
codiciar *(tr)*	covet, lust for/after **2**
coexistir *(intr)*	coexist **4**
*coger *(tr)*	take, catch, capture, hold, pick up **11**
cohabitar *(intr)*	cohabit **2**
coincidir *(intr)*	coincide **4**
cojear *(intr)*	limp **2**
colaborar *(intr)*	collaborate **2**
colar *(tr)*	sieve, sift, strain (*drain water off*) **20**
colegir *(tr)*	collect; infer **11**

colgar *(tr/intr)*	hang, hang up	**7, 20**
colmar *(tr)*	fill up	**2**
colocar *(tr)*	place	**5**
colorear *(tr)*	color	**2**
combatir *(tr)*	combat, fight	**4**
combinar(se) *(tr/refl)*	combine	**2**
comentar *(tr/intr)*	comment, remark	**2**
comenzar *(tr/intr)*	begin, start, get started	**6, 19**
***comer** *(tr/intr)*	eat, have (*to eat*)	**3**
comercializar *(tr)*	commercialize, market	**6**
comerciar *(tr/intr)*	deal, trade	**2**
cometer *(tr)*	commit	**3**
comisionar *(tr)*	commission	**2**
compadecer(se) de *(tr/refl)*	pity, sympathize, take pity on	**32**
comparar *(tr)*	compare	**2**
compartir *(tr)*	share	**4**
compensar *(tr)*	compensate	**2**
competir *(intr)*	compete; race	**24**
compilar *(tr)*	compile	**2**
completar *(tr)*	complete	**2**
complicar *(tr)*	complicate	**5**
componer *(tr)*	compose; fix	**47**
componerse de *(refl)*	be composed of, consist (*of*)	**47**
comportarse *(refl)*	behave	**2**
***comprar** *(tr)*	buy, purchase; take over (*business*)	**2**
comprender *(tr)*	comprise; understand	**2**
comprimir *(tr)*	compress	**4**
comprobar *(tr)*	check, verify	**20**
comprometerse a *(refl)*	commit oneself to	**3**
computar *(tr)*	compute	**2**
comulgar *(tr/intr)*	administer/take communion	**7**
comunicar *(tr/intr)*	communicate	**5**
concebir *(tr)*	conceive	**4**
conceder *(tr)*	allow, award (*prize*), concede, cede; confer, grant	**3**
concentrarse *(refl)*	concentrate, gather; center on	**2**

VERB INDEX

construir *(tr)*	build, construct, erect, make **12**
consultar *(tr)*	consult, go and see (e.g., *doctor*) **2**
consumir *(tr)*	consume **4**
contactar *(tr)*	contact **2**
contagiar(se) *(tr/refl)*	become infected, infect **2**
contaminar *(tr)*	contaminate, pollute **2**
contar *(tr)*	count, number; check off; relate, tell **20**
contar con *(intr)*	count on, depend on
contemplar *(tr/intr)*	contemplate, gaze at view **2**
contener(se) *(tr/refl)*	contain, hold; hold back **54**
contentar *(tr)*	please **2**
contestar *(tr)*	answer, rejoin, reply **2**
continuar *(tr/intr)*	carry on, continue **15**
contradecir(se) *(tr/refl)*	contradict (oneself) **34**
contraer(se) *(tr/refl)*	contract; shrink **55**
contrahacer *(tr)*	copy, imitate **41**
contrastar *(tr)*	contrast **2**
contratar *(tr)*	hire **2**
contravenir *(tr)*	contravene **57**
contribuir *(tr)*	contribute **12**
controlar *(tr)*	control, inspect, monitor **2**
contundir *(tr)*	bruise **4**
convencer *(tr)*	convince, bring around **9**
convenir *(tr)*	fit, suit; agree **57**
conversar *(intr)*	converse **2**
convertir *(tr)*	convert, transform **22**
convertirse en *(refl)*	turn into **22**
convidar *(tr)*	invite, treat **2**
convivir *(intr)*	coexist **4**
convocar *(tr)*	call a meeting, summon **5**
cooperar *(intr)*	cooperate **2**
coordinar *(tr)*	coordinate **2**
copiar *(tr)*	copy **2**
coquetear *(intr)*	flirt **2**
coronar *(tr)*	cap, crown **2**
corregir *(tr)*	correct **11, 24**
correr *(intr)*	run, flow, race, slip, stream **3**

corresponder *(intr)*	correspond 3
corroer(se) *(tr/refl)*	corrode, erode, rust 30
corromper(se) *(tr/refl)*	corrupt, decay, rot 3
cortar *(tr/intr)*	cut, chop, mow, slice, trim; turn off, switch off; turn out; break in (*conversation*) 2
cortejar *(tr)*	court, woo 2
cosechar *(tr)*	harvest, reap 2
coser *(tr)*	sew, stitch 3
cosquillear *(tr)*	tickle 2
costar *(intr)*	cost 20
cotizar *(tr)*	quote, price, value 6
crear *(tr)*	create 2
crecer *(intr)*	grow 32
creer *(tr)*	believe 13
crepitar *(intr)*	crackle, sizzle 2
criar *(tr)*	bring up (*children*) 14
cristalizar *(tr)*	crystallize 6
criticar *(tr)*	criticize 5
croar *(intr)*	croak 2
cronometrar *(tr)*	time 2
crucificar *(tr)*	crucify 5
crujir *(intr)*	crack, creak, crunch, rustle 4
cruzar *(tr)*	bridge, cross 6
cuadrar *(tr)*	square 2
cuantificar *(tr)*	quantity 5
cubicar *(tr)*	cube 5
cubrir *(tr)*	cover 25
cuchichear *(intr)*	whisper 2
cuestionar *(tr)*	interrogate, question 2
cuidar *(tr)*	look after, nurse, take care of 2
culpar *(tr)*	blame 2
cultivar *(tr/intr)*	cultivate, farm, grow 2
cumplir *(tr)*	carry out, fulfill, perform, keep to (*promise*) 4
curar *(tr)*	cure, heal 2
D ***dar** *(tr)*	give 33
dar los naipes *(tr)*	deal cards

dar a luz *(tr)*	give birth
dar cuerda *(tr)*	wind
dar de comer *(tr)*	feed
dar entrada *(tr)*	admit, allow in
dar fruto *(intr)*	bear fruit
dar guerra *(tr)*	bother, play up
dar gusto *(tr)*	please
dar la bienvenida *(tr)*	welcome
dar la hora *(intr)*	strike *(hour)*
dar las gracias *(tr)*	thank
dar marcha atrás *(intr)*	back, reverse *(car)*
dar razón *(tr)*	account for
dar resultado *(intr)*	give results
dar testimonio de *(tr)*	bear witness to
dar un paso *(intr)*	step
dar un puntapié *(tr)*	kick
dar un salto mortal *(intr)*	somersault
dar una palmada *(tr)*	slap
dar voces *(intr)*	call out, shout out
dar vueltas *(intr)*	circle
darse cuenta de *(refl)*	realize
darse prisa *(refl)*	hurry, make haste
datar de *(intr)*	date from **2**
deambular *(intr)*	saunter; wander **2**
debatir *(tr)*	debate **4**
deber *(tr)*	owe **3**
deber *(intr)*	have to, must, ought, should **3**
debilitar(se) *(tr/refl)*	weaken; wilt **2**
decaer *(intr)*	decay, decline **30**
decepcionar *(tr)*	disappoint **2**
decidir *(tr)*	decide **4**
decidirse *(refl)*	make up one's mind **4**
*decir *(tr/intr)*	say; tell **34**
declarar *(tr/intr)*	declare, state **2**
decorar *(tr)*	decorate **2**
decretar *(tr)*	decree **2**
dedicar *(tr)*	dedicate **5**
dedicarse a *(tr/refl)*	dedicate oneself to, devote oneself to **5**

VERB INDEX

deducir *(tr)*	deduce **31**
defender *(tr)*	champion, defend, stand up for **19**
definir *(tr)*	define **4**
deformar *(tr)*	deform **2**
defraudar *(tr)*	cheat, defraud, deceive **2**
degradar *(tr)*	degrade **2**
dejar *(tr)*	leave, let **2**
dejar caer *(tr)*	drop, let fall
dejar de lado *(tr)*	put aside
dejar de *(intr)*	stop (. . .ing)
dejar entrar *(tr)*	let in
dejar pasar *(tr)*	let by/through
dejar perplejo *(tr)*	bewilder
dejar sin sentido *(tr)*	knock out
delegar *(tr)*	delegate **7**
deleitar *(tr)*	delight **2**
deletrear *(tr)*	spell **2**
delirar *(intr)*	rave **2**
demorar(se) *(tr/refl)*	delay; take a long time **2**
demostrar *(tr)*	demonstrate, prove **20**
denominar *(tr)*	denominate **2**
denunciar *(tr)*	denounce **2**
depender de *(tr)*	depend on **3**
depositar *(tr)*	deposit **2**
depreciar *(intr)*	depreciate **2**
deprimir *(tr)*	depress **4**
depurar *(tr)*	purify; debug *(computing)* **2**
derramar(se) *(tr/intr/refl)*	leak, pour, spill **2**
derrapar *(intr)*	skid **2**
derretir(se) *(tr/intr/refl)*	melt, thaw **24**
derribar *(tr)*	demolish, knock down **2**
derrochar *(tr)*	waste **2**
derrotar *(tr)*	defeat, master **2**
derrumbarse *(refl)*	collapse **2**
desabotonar *(tr)*	unbotton **2**
desabrochar *(tr)*	unfasten **2**
desacoplar *(tr)*	uncouple **2**
desactivar *(tr)*	defuse, disarm **2**

desafiar *(tr)*	challenge 14
desagregarse *(refl)*	disintegrate 7
desaguar *(tr)*	drain 8
desalentar *(tr)*	discourage 2
desamarrar *(tr)*	cast off, untie (*boat*) 2
desamparar *(tr)*	abandon 2
desanimar *(tr)*	discourage 2
desaparecer *(intr)*	disappear, vanish 32
desaprobar *(intr)*	disapprove 20
desarmar *(tr)*	disarm 2
desarrollar(se) *(tr/refl)*	develop, evolve 2
desatar *(tr)*	undo, untie 2
desatascar *(tr)*	unblock (*commerce*) 5
desatender *(tr)*	neglect 19
desayunar *(tr/intr)*	have breakfast 2
desbloquear *(tr)*	unblock (*commerce*) 2
desbordar(se) *(intr/refl)*	flood, overflow 2
descalzar(se) *(tr/refl)*	take off (*shoes*) 6
descansar *(tr/intr)*	repose, rest 2
descargar *(tr/intr)*	discharge, download (*computing*), dump, unload 7
descascarar *(tr)*	shell (*eggs*) 2
descender *(intr)*	come down, descend, go down 19
descifrar *(tr)*	decipher, decode 2
descolgar *(tr)*	lift (*receiver*), unhook; take down 7, 20
descolorar *(intr)*	fade 2
descomponer(se) *(tr/refl)*	decompose; break down 47
desconcertar *(tr)*	embarrass, throw off balance 19
desconectar *(tr)*	disconnect, switch off, turn off 2
desconfiar de *(tr)*	distrust 14
descongelar *(tr)*	defrost, thaw, deice 2
desconocer *(tr)*	be ignorant; deny 32
descontar *(tr)*	deduct, discount 20
describir *(tr)*	describe 37
descubrir *(tr)*	discover, find out, strike (*oil*), uncover 25

descuidar *(tr)*	neglect **2**
desdecir(se) *(tr/refl)*	clash with; withdraw **34**
desdeñar *(tr)*	scorn **2**
desear *(tr)*	desire, want, wish **2**
desechar *(tr)*	throw away **2**
desembalar *(tr)*	unpack **2**
desembarazarse de *(refl)*	rid, rid oneself of **6**
desembarcar *(intr)*	disembark, land **5**
desembocar en *(intr)*	flow into **5**
desembolsar *(tr)*	pay out **2**
desempolvar *(tr)*	dust **2**
desenganchar *(tr)*	uncouple, unhook **2**
desenredar *(tr)*	disentangle **2**
desenterrar *(tr)*	dig up, unearth **19**
desenvainar *(tr)*	draw (*sword*); shell (*peas*) **2**
desertar *(tr)*	desert **19**
desesperar *(intr)*	despair **2**
desfigurar *(tr)*	disfigure, deface **2**
desgarrar *(tr)*	tear **2**
desguazar *(tr)*	scrap **2**
deshacer *(tr)*	undo; ruin;
	unpack (*suitcase*) **41**
deshacerse de *(refl)*	dispense with, dump, get rid of
deshelar *(tr)*	defrost, deice **19**
deshelar(se) *(tr/refl)*	thaw
desherbar *(tr)*	weed **19**
desheredar *(tr)*	disinherit **2**
deshollinar *(tr)*	sweep (*chimney*) **2**
designar *(tr)*	designate **2**
desilusionar *(tr)*	disappoint **2**
desinfectar *(tr)*	disinfect **2**
desinflar *(tr)*	deflate **2**
desintegrar(se) *(intr/refl)*	disintegrate **2**
deslizarse *(intr)*	creep, slide **6**
deslumbrar *(tr)*	dazzle **2**
desmaquillar(se) *(tr/refl)*	remove makeup **2**
desmayar *(intr)*	faint **2**
desmentir *(tr)*	refute **22**
desmenuzar(se) *(intr/refl)*	crumble **6**

desmigajar(se) *(tr/refl)*	crumble 2
desmontar *(tr)*	dismantle (e.g., *tent*), take down 2
desmoronarse *(refl)*	fall apart 2
desnudar(se) *(tr/refl)*	bare, strip off, undress 2
desobedecer *(tr/intr)*	disobey 32
desobstruir *(tr)*	unblock 12
desoír *(tr)*	ignore, turn a deaf ear to 44
desollar *(tr)*	skin 20
desorganizar *(tr)*	disorganize 6
despachar *(tr)*	dispatch, send off 2
desparramarse *(refl)*	scatter 2
despedir *(tr)*	dismiss, fire 24
despedir(se) *(tr/refl)*	say good-bye to, take leave of 24
despegar *(tr/intr)*	lift off (*rocket*), take off; take down (e.g., *poster*); detach, unstick 7
despejar(se) *(tr/refl)*	brighten up, clear 2
despellejar *(tr)*	skin 2
despertar(se) *(tr/refl)*	awaken, wake up 19
despilfarrar *(tr)*	waste 2
desplazar *(tr)*	displace 6
desplazar hacia arriba *(tr)*	scroll up
desplazar hacia abajo *(tr)*	scroll down
desplegar *(tr)*	display 7, 19
despojar(se) de *(tr/refl)*	take away from; shed, take off 2
despreciar *(tr)*	scorn 2
destacar(se) *(tr/refl)*	be noticeable, highlight; stand out 5
destapar *(tr)*	uncover 2
destellar *(intr)*	flash, sparkle 2
desterrar *(tr)*	banish, exile 19
destilar *(tr)*	distill 2
destornillar *(tr)*	unscrew 2
destruir *(tr)*	destroy 12
desvalorizar *(tr)*	devalue 6
desviar *(intr)*	divert 14
desviar(se) de *(refl)*	detour, deviate, skew 14

detallar *(tr)*	detail **2**
detectar *(tr)*	detect **2**
detener(se) *(tr/refl)*	stop; arrest, detain **54**
deteriorar *(intr)*	deteriorate **2**
determinar *(tr)*	determine **2**
detestar *(tr)*	detest, hate **2**
devaluar *(tr)*	devalue **15**
devastar *(tr)*	devastate **2**
devolver *(tr)*	give back, hand back, pay back; return, send back, take back (*goods*) **20**
devolverse *(refl)*	go back **20**
devorar *(tr)*	devour **2**
diagnosticar *(tr)*	diagnose **5**
dibujar *(tr)*	draw **2**
dictar *(tr)*	dictate **2**
difamar *(tr)*	slander **2**
diferenciar *(tr)*	differentiate **2**
diferenciarse *(refl)*	be different **2**
diferir *(intr)*	differ **22**
dificultar *(tr)*	hinder **2**
difundir *(tr)*	diffuse, spread **4**
digerir *(tr)*	digest **22**
dignarse *(refl)*	deign to **2**
diluir *(tr)*	dilute **12**
dimitir *(tr)*	resign **4**
diputar *(tr)*	delegate, deputize **2**
dirigir *(tr)*	address (e.g., *letter*); direct, manage, steer **11**
dirigirse a/hacia *(refl)*	address (*a person*)/make for, head for **11**
discernir *(tr)*	discern **19**
disciplinar *(tr)*	discipline **2**
disculpar *(tr)*	excuse, exonerate; forgive **2**
disculparse *(refl)*	apologize **2**
discutir *(tr/intr)*	argue, debate, discuss **4**
diseminar *(tr)*	disseminate, spread **2**
diseñar *(tr)*	design, style **2**
disfrazar *(tr)*	disguise **6**

disfrutar *(tr)*	enjoy **2**
disgregarse *(refl)*	disintegrate **7**
disimular *(tr)*	conceal; pretend **2**
dislocarse *(refl)*	dislocate **5**
disminuir *(tr/intr)*	diminish, decrease, lessen **12**
disolver(se) *(tr/refl)*	dissolve **20**
disparar *(tr/intr)*	fire, shoot **2**
dispensar *(tr)*	exempt, pardon **2**
dispersar(se) *(tr/refl)*	disperse, scatter **2**
disponer de *(tr)*	dispose of; have available **47**
disputar *(tr/intr)*	argue, dispute **2**
***distinguir** *(tr)*	distinguish, make out, differentiate **10**
distinguir entre *(tr)*	tell (apart)
distinguirse *(refl)*	excel **10**
distraer *(tr)*	distract **55**
distribuir *(tr)*	distribute **12**
disuadir *(tr)*	dissuade **4**
divagar *(intr)*	ramble on, waffle **7**
divertir *(tr)*	amuse, divert, entertain **22**
divertirse *(refl)*	enjoy oneself **22**
dividir *(tr)*	divide **4**
divisar *(tr)*	make out, sight **2**
divorciar(se) *(tr/refl)*	divorce, get divorced **2**
divulgar *(tr)*	divulge, spread **2**
doblar(se) *(tr/refl)*	double; fold, fold up; bend down, bend over **2**
doler *(tr/intr)*	ache, distress, hurt, pain **20**
domar *(tr)*	tame **2**
domesticar *(tr)*	tame **5**
dominar *(tr)*	master *(a subject)*; overlook **2**
dominarse *(refl)*	control oneself **2**
donar *(tr)*	donate **2**
***dormir(se)** *(intr/refl)*	sleep; fall asleep **23**
drogar *(tr)*	dope, drug **7**
drogarse *(refl)*	take drugs
duchar(se) *(tr/refl)*	shower **2**
dudar *(tr)*	doubt **2**
duplicar *(tr)*	double; duplicate **5**

	durar *(tr/intr)*	hold out, last **2**
E	echar *(tr)*	pour; sprout; cast, toss, throw, throw away **2**
	echar de menos *(tr)*	miss (*somebody*)
	echar la culpa *(tr)*	blame
	echar un vistazo *(intr)*	glance
	echar vapor *(intr)*	steam
	echarse *(refl)*	lie (down) **2**
	echarse atrás *(refl)*	back down
	economizar *(tr)*	economize **6**
	editar *(tr)*	edit **2**
	educar *(tr)*	educate **5**
	efectuar *(tr)*	bring about **15**
	ejecutar *(tr)*	execute, realize; carry out; run *(computing)* **2**
	ejercer *(tr)*	exercise; exert; practice **9**
	ejercitarse *(refl)*	exercise **2**
	elaborar *(tr)*	elaborate, make; work out *(plan)* **2**
	electrificar *(tr)*	electrify **5**
	elegir *(tr)*	choose, elect, pick; vote **11, 24**
	elevar *(tr)*	elevate, heighten **2**
	eliminar *(tr)*	eliminate **2**
	elogiar *(tr)*	praise **2**
	embarcar(se) *(tr/refl)*	board, embark, ship **5**
	embellecer *(tr)*	beautify, embellish **32**
	embestir *(tr)*	assault, charge **24**
	emborracharse *(intr)*	get drunk **2**
	embotellar *(tr)*	bottle **2**
	embromar *(tr)*	tease **2**
	emigrar *(tr)*	emigrate **2**
	emitir *(tr)*	broadcast, emit, issue **4**
	emocionar *(tr)*	excite, move **2**
	empapar *(tr)*	soak, steep **2**
	empapelar *(tr)*	paper **2**
	empaquetar *(tr)*	package **2**
	emparejar *(tr)*	match **2**
	empastar *(tr)*	fill *(a tooth)* **2**

empatar *(intr)*	tie *(in sport)* **2**
empeorar *(intr)*	get worse, worsen **2**
empezar *(tr/intr)*	begin, get started, start **6, 19**
emplastar *(tr)*	plaster *(medical)* **2**
emplazar *(tr)*	place, site **6**
emplear *(tr)*	employ, use **2**
empollar *(tr)*	incubate, sit on **2**
empotrar *(tr)*	build in **2**
emprender *(tr)*	take on, take up, undertake **3**
empujar *(tr/intr)*	push; prod, shove **2**
emulsionar *(tr)*	emulsify **2**
enajenar *(tr)*	alienate **2**
enamorar(se) de *(tr/refl)*	fall in love with **2**
encadenar *(tr)*	chain up **2**
encajonar *(tr)*	box up **2**
encanecer *(intr)*	go gray **32**
encantar *(tr)*	charm, enchant **2**
encarar *(tr)*	confront **2**
encarcelar *(tr)*	imprison **2**
encargar *(tr)*	commission, order **7**
encauzar *(tr)*	channel **6**
encender(se) *(tr/refl)*	turn on; light, ignite, strike *(match)* **19**
encerrar *(tr)*	confine, enclose, shut in **19**
enclavijar *(tr)*	peg **2**
encoger(se) *(tr/refl)*	flinch, shrink **11**
encogerse de hombros *(rcfl)*	shrug
encontrar(se) *(tr/refl)*	find; meet, run into **20**
encorvar(se) *(tr/refl)*	bend over, stoop, curve **2**
enderezar(se) *(tr/refl)*	straighten **6**
endosar *(tr)*	endorse **2**
endulzar *(tr)*	sweeten **6**
endurecer(se) *(tr/refl)*	harden **32**
enfadar(se) *(tr/refl)*	anger, annoy; get annoyed **2**
enfermar(se) *(intr/refl)*	fall ill, sick **2**
enfrascar *(tr)*	bottle; get involved **5**
enfrentarse *(refl)*	confront, face up **2**
enfriar *(tr)*	cool down **14**
enfurecer *(tr)*	enrage, madden **32**

enganchar *(tr)*	hook; harness (*horse to a cart*) **2**
engañar *(tr)*	bluff, deceive, fool, trick **2**
engordar *(tr/intr)*	fatten **2**
engrasar *(tr)*	grease **2**
engullir *(tr)*	guzzle, swallow **16**
enhebrar *(tr)*	thread **19**
enjabonar *(tr)*	soap **2**
enjaezar *(tr)*	harness **6**
enjuagar *(tr)*	rinse **7**
enjugar *(tr)*	dry, wipe **2, 21**
enlazar *(tr)*	bind, tie **6**
enlazar con *(tr)*	link with
enloquecer *(tr)*	madden **32**
enlucir *(tr)*	plaster **43**
enmarcar *(tr)*	frame **5**
enmendar *(tr)*	amend **19**
enmohecer(se)	get moldy **32**
ennegrecer(se) *(tr/refl)*	blacken **32**
enojar(se) *(tr/refl)*	anger; annoy, get angry **2**
enriquecer *(tr)*	enrich **32**
enrollar *(tr/intr)*	coil, roll open **2**
ensanchar *(tr)*	broaden, enlarge, widen **2**
ensartar *(tr)*	string (*together*), thread **2**
ensayar *(tr)*	rehearse, try **2**
enseñar *(tr/intr)*	show; teach **2**
ensillar *(tr)*	saddle **2**
ensordecer *(tr)*	deafen **32**
ensortijar *(tr)*	curl **2**
ensuciar(se) *(tr/refl)*	dirty, soil **2**
entender *(tr)*	understand **19**
enterrar *(tr)*	bury **19**
entrampar *(tr)*	trap **2**
entrar *(tr/intr)*	enter, get in, go in, go into **2**
entrar en un fichero *(tr)*	access (*a file*)
entrar violentamente *(intr)*	burst in
entreabrir *(tr)*	half open **25**
entregar *(tr)*	deliver, hand in; turn over, yield **7**

entregar(se) *(tr/refl)*	surrender	**7**
entregarse a *(refl)*	become addicted	**7**
entrenar *(tr)*	train	**2**
entrenarse *(refl)*	get fit, train	**2**
entretener *(tr)*	entertain	**54**
entretenerse *(refl)*	amuse oneself	**54**
entrever *(tr)*	glimpse	**58**
entrevistar *(tr)*	interview	**2**
entristecer *(tr)*	sadden	**32**
entusiasmar *(tr)*	enthuse, excite	**2**
envasar *(tr)*	package	**2**
envejecer *(intr)*	age	**32**
envenenar *(tr)*	poison	**2**
***enviar** *(tr)*	send	**14**
enviar por *(tr)*	send for	
enviar por correo *(tr)*	mail, post	
enviciarse con	become addicted to	**2**
envidiar *(tr)*	envy	**2**
envilecer *(tr)*	degrade	**32**
envolver *(tr)*	wrap up	**20**
enyesar *(tr)*	plaster	**2**
equilibrar(se) *(tr/refl)*	balance; break even	**2**
equipar de *(tr)*	equip, outfit	**2**
equiparar *(tr)*	match	**2**
equivocar *(tr)*	mistake someone for	**5**
equivocarse *(refl)*	be wrong, be mistaken	**5**
***erguir(se)** *(tr/refl)*	raise; lift; straighten up	**35**
erigir *(tr)*	erect; rear	**11**
erosionar *(tr)*	erode	**2**
***errar** *(intr)*	stray; wander; err	**36**
esbozar *(tr)*	sketch out	**6**
escabullirse *(refl)*	break off, slip away	**16**
escalar *(tr)*	climb, scale	**2**
escapar(se) *(refl)*	escape, run away	**2**
escardar *(tr)*	weed	**2**
esclarecer *(intr)*	clear up	**32**
esclavizar *(tr)*	enslave	**6**
escocer *(tr)*	sting	**9, 20**
escoger *(tr)*	choose, select	**11**

esconder(se) *(tr/refl)*	hide	3
*escribir *(tr)*	write	37
escribir a máquina *(tr)*	type	
escuchar *(tr)*	listen	2
escuchar clandestinamente *(tr)*	bug	2
escudriñar *(tr)*	scrutinize; search	2
escupir *(intr)*	spit	4
escurrir *(tr)*	wring	4
esforzarse *(refl)*	make an effort, strain, struggle, try	6, 20
esgrimir *(intr)*	fence (*sport*)	4
esnifar *(tr)*	sniff	2
espabilar la borrachera *(intr)*	sober up	2
espantar *(tr)*	frighten, scare	2
esparcir *(tr)*	scatter; sow	9
especificar *(tr)*	specify	5
especializar *(intr)*	specialize	6
especular *(tr/intr)*	gamble, speculate	2
esperar *(tr/intr)*	wait, hope; expect	2
espesar(se) *(tr/refl)*	thicken	2
espiar *(intr)*	spy	14
espumar *(intr)*	foam	2
esquiar *(intr)*	ski	2
esquilar *(tr)*	clip, shear	2
estabilizar(se) *(tr/refl)*	stabilize, steady	6
establecer *(tr)*	establish, set up	32
establecerse *(refl)*	settle	32
establecerse sin derecho *(refl)*	squat	
estacionar *(tr)*	park	2
estafar *(tr)*	cheat, deceive, take in, trick	2
estallar *(intr)*	explode, blow up	2
*estar *(intr)*	be	38
estar a favor de	be for (*support*)	
estar a punto de	be about to	
estar a régimen	be on a diet	
estar aburrido	be bored	
estar adelantado	be fast (*clock*)	
estar amohinado	sulk, be irritated	

estar asustado	be scared
estar atrasado	be slow (*clock*)
estar ausente	be absent
estar avergonzado	be ashamed
estar bloqueado	be stuck
estar contento	be happy
estar de acuerdo	agree with
estar de luto	mourn, be in mourning
estar descontento	be unhappy
estar desempleado	be unemployed
estar emparentado con	be related to
estar en contra de	be against
estar enfadado	be angry
estar enojado	be annoyed
estar equivocado	be mistaken
estar estreñido	be constipated
estar ilusionado	be looking forward to
estar insatisfecho	be dissatisfied
estar interesado en	be interested in
estar mareado	be dizzy
estar ocupado	be busy
estar parado	be unemployed
estar plagado de	be crawling with
estar pluriempleado	moonlight
estar presente sin intervenir	stand by
estar separado	be separated
estar situado	be situated
estimar (tr)	estimate, quote; prize, rate (*evaluate*), value **2**
estirar(se) (tr/refl)	stretch; strain; extend; tighten **2**
estorbar (tr)	hinder, thwart **2**
estornudar (intr)	sneeze **2**
estrangular (tr)	strangle, throttle **2**
estrechar(se) (tr/refl)	extend, hold out; narrow; tighten **2**
estrellar (intr)	crash **2**
estremecerse (refl)	quiver, shiver, shudder **32**

VERB INDEX

estrenar *(tr)*	release (*film*, etc.); open (*show*); wear for the first time **2**
estropear *(tr)*	harm, ruin, spoil **2**
estructurar *(tr)*	structure **2**
estudiar *(tr/intr)*	study **2**
etiquetar *(tr)*	label **2**
evacuar *(tr)*	evacuate **2**
evadir(se) *(tr/refl)*	dodge, evade, run away **2**
evaluar *(tr)*	appraise, evaluate **2**
evitar *(tr)*	avoid **2**
evocar *(tr)*	evoke **5**
evolucionar *(tr)*	evolve **2**
exagerar *(tr)*	exaggerate **2**
examinar *(tr)*	check, examine **2**
exasperar *(tr)*	exasperate **2**
excavar *(tr)*	dig, hollow out **2**
exceder *(tr)*	exceed, surpass, top **3**
exceptuar *(tr)*	except **15**
excitar *(tr)*	excite, work up (*interest, emotion*, etc.) **2**
exclamar *(tr)*	exclaim **2**
excluir *(tr)*	exclude **12**
exculpar *(tr)*	exonerate **2**
exhalar *(tr)*	exhale **2**
exhibir *(tr)*	exhibit **4**
exigir *(tr)*	demand; require **11**
existir *(intr)*	exist **4**
expedir *(tr)*	dispatch, send off **24**
experimentar *(tr)*	experience, feel; experiment **2**
expirar *(tr)*	expire **2**
explicar *(tr)*	explain, give reasons **5**
explorar *(tr)*	explore **2**
explosionar *(intr)*	blow up, explode **2**
explotar *(tr/intr)*	blow up, explode, set off (*explosion*) **2**
exponer *(tr)*	display, expose **47**
exportar *(tr)*	export **2**
expresar *(tr)*	express **2**
exprimir *(tr)*	squeeze (*out*), wring **4**

extender(se) *(tr/efl)*	stretch, extend, spread; expand: lay out **19**
extender la mano	reach out for
extinguir *(tr)*	extinguish **10**
extraer *(tr)*	extract **55**
extraer minerales *(tr)*	mine
extrañar *(tr)*	find strange; miss **2**
extraviarse *(refl)*	stray **14**
F **fabricar** *(tr)*	make, manufacture **5**
facilitar *(tr)*	facilitate; provide supply **2**
facturar *(tr)*	bill; check in (*baggage*) **2**
fallar *(intr)*	fail, miss **2**
falsificar *(tr)*	fake **5**
faltar *(Intr)*	be missing lack; fail, let down **2**
fascinar *(tr)*	fascinate **2**
fastidiar *(tr)*	get on someone's nerves, tease **2**
fatigar(se) *(tr/refl)*	tire **7**
favorecer *(tr)*	favor **32**
felicitar *(tr)*	congratulate; compliment **2**
fermentar *(tr/intr)*	ferment **2**
festejar *(tr)*	celebrate, fete **2**
fiarse de *(refl)*	trust **14**
fichar *(tr)*	file; index **2**
fichar (la entrada) *(intr)*	clock in
fichar (la salida) *(intr)*	clock out
fijar *(tr)*	fasten, fix, secure **2**
filmar *(tr)*	film, shoot (*film*) **2**
filtrar(se) *(tr/refl)*	filter, seep **2**
financiar *(tr)*	finance **2**
fingir *(tr/intr)*	fake, feign, pretend **11**
firmar *(tr)*	sign **2**
fletar *(tr)*	charter (*plane, boat*) **2**
flirtear *(intr)*	flirt **2**
florecer *(intr)*	bloom, flourish, flower **32**
flotar *(intr)*	float, hover **2**
fluir *(intr)*	flow, stream **12**
fondear *(intr)*	anchor **2**

VERB INDEX

forjar *(tr)*	fashion, form	**2**
formar *(tr)*	fashion, form, shape, train, break someone of a habit	**2**
fortalecer *(tr)*	strengthen	**32**
forzar *(tr)*	compel, force	**6, 20**
forzar la entrada *(intr)*	break in	**6**
fotocopiar *(tr)*	(photo)copy, duplicate	**2**
fotografiar *(tr)*	photograph, shoot	**14**
fracasar *(intr)*	fail	**2**
fracturar(se) *(tr/intr)*	fracture	**2**
franquear *(tr)*	frank	**2**
frecuentar *(tr)*	frequent	**2**
fregar *(tr)*	scrub, wash up	**7, 19**
***freír** *(tr)*	fry	**39**
frenar *(intr)*	brake	**2**
friccionar *(tr)*	rub	**2**
frotar *(tr)*	rub	**2**
fruncir(se) *(tr/refl)*	wrinkle	**9**
frustrar *(tr)*	frustrate	**2**
fugarse *(intr)*	flee	**7**
fumar *(tr/intr)*	smoke	**2**
funcionar *(intr)*	function, work	**2**
fundar *(tr)*	found	**2**
fundir(se) *(tr/refl)*	blow (*fuse*), fuse, melt	**4**
fusionar(se) *(tr/refl)*	fuse; merge	**2**

G

ganar *(tr/intr)*	earn; win	**2**
gandulear *(intr)*	idle	**2**
garantizar *(tr)*	guarantee, secure	**6**
garrapatear *(intr)*	scribble	**2**
gastar *(tr)*	spend (*money*); use up; wear out	**2**
gemir *(intr)*	groan, moan	**24**
generar *(tr)*	generate	**2**
girar *(tr/intr)*	gyrate, orbit, spin, turn, wheel	**2**
gobernar *(tr/intr)*	govern; steer (*ship*)	**19**
golpear *(tr)*	hit, knock, strike	**2**
gorjear *(intr)*	sing (*birds*), twitter	**2**
gotear *(intr)*	drip, trickle	**2**

gozar *(tr)*	enjoy **6**
grabar *(tr)*	engrave; record, tape; save (*computing*) **2**
graduarse *(refl)*	graduate, qualify **15**
granizar *(intr)*	hail (stones) **6**
grapar *(tr)*	staple **2**
graznar *(intr)*	croak, squawk **2**
gritar *(tr/intr)*	call out, shout **2**
***gruñir** *(intr)*	grunt, growl **17**
guardar *(tr)*	guard, watch (over); keep, store, put away (safely) **2**
guiar *(tr)*	guide, steer **14**
guiñar *(tr)*	wink **2**
gustar *(tr)*	please (used for *like*) **2**

H

***haber** *(intr)*	have (auxiliary) **40**
hablar *(tr/Intr)*	talk, speak (*language*) **2**
hablar claro *(intr)*	speak out
hablar mal de *(tr)*	speak ill of
***hacer** *(tr)*	do; make **41**
hacer abandonar una costumbre *(tr)*	break someone of a habit
hacer aparecer *(tr)*	conjure up
hacer autostop *(intr)*	hitchhike
hacer callar *(tr)*	silence
hacer camping *(intr)*	camp
hacer circular *(tr)*	circulate
hacer cola *(intr)*	get in line, queue
hacer compras *(intr)*	go shopping
hacer constar *(tr)*	minute, take minutes
hacer contrabando *(tr)*	smuggle
hacer daño *(tr)*	harm
hacer desaparecer *(tr)*	conjure (*make disappear*)
hacer eco *(intr)*	echo
hacer el amor *(intr)*	make love
hacer estallar *(tr)*	trigger off
hacer falta *(tr)*	be necessary (*lack*)
hacer frente *(tr)*	confront, cope with
hacer funcionar *(tr)*	make (something) work; run

hacer gala de *(tr)*	show off
hacer gimnasia *(intr)*	do gymnastics
hacer girar *(tr)*	wheel, turn
hacer las maletas	pack suitcases
hacer magia *(intr)*	conjure
hacer mal a *(tr)*	damage, hurt
hacer pasar *(tr)*	show in
hacer turnos *(intr)*	take turns
hacer prisionero *(tr)*	take prisoner
hacer proyectos *(intr)*	make plans
hacer punto *(intr)*	knit
hacer que uno pierda el equilibrio	throw off balance
hacer rodar *(tr)*	roll, wheel
hacer trampas *(intr)*	cheat
hacer trasbordo *(intr)*	change (trains); transfer
hacer tropezar *(tr)*	trip up
hacer una huelga *(intr)*	go on strike
hacer una pausa *(tr)*	pause
hacerse (*refl*)	become (*prospects, existence*) **41**
hacerse a la vela	sail
hacerse mayor	grow up
hacer(se) amigos *(tr/refl)*	become friends
hacer(se) borroso *(tr/refl)*	become blurred
halagar *(tr)*	coax, flatter **7**
helar(se) *(tr/refl)*	chill, ice, freeze **19**
hender(se) *(tr/refl)*	split **19**
heredar *(tr/intr)*	inherit, succeed **2**
herir *(tr)*	hurt, injure, wound **22**
herrar *(tr)*	shoe (*horse*) **19**
hervir *(tr/intr)*	boil **22**
hesitar *(intr)*	hesitate **2**
hilar *(tr)*	spin, twine **2**
hinchar *(tr)*	inflate, swell **2**
hipotecar *(tr)*	mortgage **5**
hojear *(tr)*	browse, leaf through **2**
hospedar *(tr)*	accommodate, house, lodge, put up **2**

hospedarse *(refl)*	stay (*as a guest*) 2
***huir** *(tr/intr)*	flee; run away 12
humedecer *(tr)*	dampen, moisten, wet 32
humillar *(tr)*	humiliate 2
hundir(se) *(tr/intr/refl)*	sink, subside 4
hurgar *(tr)*	poke 7
husmear *(tr)*	sniff out 2

I

idealizar *(tr)*	idealize 6
idear *(tr)*	devise, think out 2
identificar *(tr)*	identify 5
ignorar *(tr)*	ignore 2
igualar *(tr/intr)*	equal, equalize, even out 2
iluminar *(tr)*	illuminate, light (up) 2
ilustrar *(tr)*	illustrate 2
imaginar(se) *(tr/refl)*	imagine; devise, think out 2
imitar *(tr)*	imitate 2
impacientarse *(refl)*	get impatient 2
impedir *(tr)*	hinder, prevent, stop, thwart 24
implicar *(tr)*	involve 5
imponer *(tr)*	impose 47
imponer contribuciones	tax
importar *(tr)*	import 2
importar *(intr)*	be important, import, matter 2
importunar *(tr)*	disturb, pester 2
impresionar *(tr/intr)*	impress; strike 2
imprimir *(tr)*	print 4
impulsar *(tr)*	impel 2
incapacitar *(tr)*	incapacitate 2
incendiar(se) *(tr/refl)*	ignite 2
incinerar *(tr)*	cremate, incinerate 2
incitar *(tr)*	urge 2
inclinar(se) *(tr/refl)*	bow, nod; bend, lean, stoop; slope 2
incluir *(tr)*	include 12
incorporar(se) *(tr/refl)*	incorporate; join; sit up (*from lying*), get up (*from reclining position*) 2
indicar *(tr)*	indicate, point (out/to), show 5

intoxicar *(tr)*	intoxicate, poison **5**
intrigar *(intr)*	plot **7**
introducir *(tr)*	introduce, bring in; insert; enter *(computing)* **31**
introducir poco a poco *(tr)*	phase in
inundar *(tr)*	flood **2**
inventar *(tr)*	invent, make up **2**
invertir *(tr)*	invert, reverse, turn around; invest **22**
investigar *(tr)*	investigate, research **2**
invitar *(tr)*	invite, treat **2**
involucrar *(tr)*	involve **2**
inyectar *(tr)*	inject **2**
ionizar *(tr)*	ionize **6**
*ir *(intr)*	go **42**
ir a	be going to
ir a buscar	go for, go to fetch
ir a caballo *(intr)*	go on a horse, ride a horse
ir bien *(intr)*	fit; suit
ir de compras *(intr)*	go shopping, shop
ir de excursión a pie *(intr)*	hike
ir de prisa *(intr)*	hurry, rush
ir de tiendas *(intr)*	go shopping, shop
ir en bicicleta *(intr)*	cycle, go on a bike, ride a bike
ir más despacio *(intr)*	slow down
irse *(refl)*	go away, leave **42**
irse volando *(refl)*	fly away
irritar *(tr)*	irritate **2**
J jabonar *(tr)*	soap **2**
jactarse *(refl)*	boast **2**
jadear *(intr)*	gasp, pant **2**
jubilar(se) *(tr/refl)*	retire **2**
*jugar *(intr)*	play; gamble **21**
jugar el papel de *(intr)*	act out, play a role
juntar(se) *(tr/refl)*	couple, join, pool (resources); assemble, unite **2**
jurar *(tr/intr)*	swear **2**
justificar *(tr)*	justify **5**

juzgar *(tr)*	judge, prosecute, try	**7**
juzgar mal *(tr)*	misjudge	

L

labrar *(tr)*	cultivate, farm, till	**2**
ladear *(tr)*	skirt around; incline	**2**
ladrar *(intr)*	bark	**2**
lamentar *(tr/intr)*	be sorry, lament, regret	**2**
lamer *(tr)*	lick	**4**
languidecer *(intr)*	languish, pine (away)	**32**
lanzar *(tr)*	bowl, cast, launch, throw	**6**
largar(se) de *(tr/refl)*	clear off, clear out,	
	get out of way of, go away	**7**
lastimar *(tr)*	damage, hurt	**2**
latir *(intr)*	beat (*heart*)	**4**
lavar(se) *(tr/refl)*	wash	**2**
***leer** *(tr/intr)*	read	**13**
leer en voz alta *(tr)*	read aloud	
legalizar *(tr)*	legalize	**6**
legar *(tr)*	bequeath, leave	**7**
legitimar *(tr)*	legalize	**2**
levantar *(tr)*	hoist, lift, raise; erect, rear	**2**
levantar los ojos	look up	
levantarse *(refl)*	get up, stand up	**2**
liar *(tr)*	bind, bond, tie	**14**
libertar *(tr)*	free, set free	**2**
librar(se) de *(tr/refl)*	rid, rid oneself of	**2**
licenciar *(tr)*	license	**2**
licitar *(tr)*	bid	**2**
lijar *(tr)*	sandpaper	**2**
limar *(tr)*	file down	**2**
limitar *(tr)*	limit	**2**
limpiar *(tr)*	clean, polish; tidy up, wipe	**2**
lindar *(tr)*	border	**2**
liquidar *(tr)*	liquidate; pay off, sell cheaply	**2**
lisonjear *(tr)*	flatter	**2**
llamar *(tr)*	call, name, summon, term;	
	send for	**2**
llamar a *(intr)*	call to, hail	
llamar a filas *(tr)*	call up	

llamar con señas *(tr)*	beckon
llamar por teléfono *(tr)*	call, ring (up), (tele)phone
llamear *(intr)*	flare **2**
llegar *(intr)*	arrive; come round (*date*, etc.), reach **7**
llegar tarde	be late
llenar *(tr)*	cram, fill, pack, stuff **2**
llevar *(tr)*	bear, carry; take, transfer; convey; drive someone; have on, wear **2**
llevar a cabo *(tr)*	accomplish, carry out, implement
llevar la batuta *(intr)*	conduct (*orchestra*); be in control
llevar la delantera *(intr)*	lead
llevarse *(refl)*	take out/away (*including food*); get away with; carry off, remove **2**
lleverse bien con *(tr)*	get along with, get on well
llorar *(intr)*	cry, mourn, weep **2**
llover *(intr)*	rain **20**
lloviznar *(intr)*	drizzle **2**
lograr *(tr/intr)*	achieve **2**
lubricar *(tr)*	lubricate **5**
lubrificar *(tr)*	lubricate, oil **5**
luchar *(tr/intr)*	fight, struggle, wrestle **2**
*lucir(se) *(tr/intr/refl)*	shine; excel; show off **43**

M

machacar *(tr)*	mash, pound **5**
madurar *(tr/intr)*	ripen **2**
magnetizar *(tr)*	magnetize **6**
maldecir *(tr)*	curse, damn **28**
malear(se) *(tr/refl)*	sour **2**
malgastar *(tr)*	waste **2**
malinterpretar *(tr)*	misinterpret **2**
malparir *(intr)*	miscarry **4**
maltratar *(tr)*	abuse, maltreat, mistreat **2**
malversar *(tr)*	embezzle **2**
mamar *(tr)*	suckle **2**
manar *(intr)*	flow, well up **2**
manchar(se) *(tr/refl)*	soil, spot, stain **2**

merendar en el campo *(intr)*	picnic **19**
meter *(tr)*	put in, stock **3**
mezclar *(tr/intr)*	blend, jumble up, mix **2**
migrar *(intr)*	migrate **2**
mimar *(tr)*	spoil (*child*) **2**
mirar *(tr/intr)*	gaze, look (at), watch, view **2**
mirar boquiabierto *(tr)*	gape at
mirar fijamente *(tr)*	stare
mirar furtivamente *(tr)*	peep
mirar rápidamente *(tr)*	peep
modelar *(tr)*	model **2**
moderar la marcha *(intr)*	slow down, draw in **2**
modernizar *(tr)*	modernize, update **6**
modificar *(tr)*	modify, vary **5**
mojar *(tr)*	dampen, dip, moisten, soak, wet **2**
moldear *(tr)*	mold, shape **2**
moler *(tr)*	grind, mill **20**
molestar *(tr)*	bother, disturb, molest, pester **2**
molestar(se) *(tr/refl)*	trouble; get angry **2**
mondar *(tr)*	peel **2**
monopolizar *(tr)*	monopolize **6**
montar *(tr)*	assemble, erect; mount **2**
montar *(en) (tr/intr)*	ride
montar a caballo *(intr)*	go horse riding
morder *(tr)*	bite **20**
mordiscar *(tr/intr)*	nibble **5**
morir *(intr)*	die **23**
morir de hambre *(intr)*	starve (*to death*)
mortificar *(tr)*	spite **5**
mostrar *(tr)*	show **20**
motivar *(tr)*	motivate **2**
mover(se) *(tr/refl)*	move; wag **20**
mudar(se) *(tr/refl)*	change; molt; move house **2**
muestrear *(tr)*	sample **2**
multar *(tr)*	fine **2**
multiplicar(se) *(tr/refl)*	multiply **5**
murmullar *(tr/intr)*	murmur **2**

	mutilar *(tr)*	mutilate **2**
N	**nacer** *(intr)*	be born **32**
	nadar *(intr)*	swim **2**
	narrar *(tr)*	narrate, relate, report **2**
	naufragar *(tr/intr)*	be shipwrecked, sink **7**
	navegar *(tr)*	navigate, sail **7**
	necesitar *(tr)*	need, require **2**
	negar *(tr)*	deny, disclaim **7, 19**
	negociar con *(tr/intr)*	negotiate; do business with **2**
	neutralizar *(tr)*	neutralize **6**
	nevar *(intr)*	snow **19**
	nombrar *(tr)*	appoint, engage, nominate; name **2**
	normalizar *(tr)*	standardize **6**
	notar *(tr)*	note, remark; notice, see, spot **2**
	nublarse *(refl)*	cloud over **2**
	nutrir *(tr)*	feed, nourish **4**
O	**obedecer** *(tr)*	obey **32**
	obligar *(tr)*	compel, constrain, force, oblige **7**
	obrar (de acuerdo con) *(intr)*	act (on) **2**
	obsequiar *(tr)*	give away (*as a present*), present with **2**
	observar *(tr)*	look at, observe, watch; remark **2**
	obstruir *(tr)*	block, obstruct **12**
	obtener *(tr)*	get, obtain **54**
	ocasionar *(tr)*	bring about, cause **2**
	ocultar(se) *(tr/refl)*	conceal, hide **2**
	ocupar *(tr)*	live in, occupy; take up (*space*) **2**
	ocuparse de *(refl)*	deal with; look after **2**
	ocuparse en *(refl)*	busy oneself **2**
	ocuparse en fruslerías	putter
	ocurrir *(intr)*	happen, occur **4**
	ocurrírsele a uno	occur to (have an idea)

odiar *(tr)*	hate **2**
ofender *(tr)*	offend **19**
ofrecer *(tr)*	offer; bid **32**
***oír** *(tr/intr)*	hear; listen; pay attention **44**
***oler** *(tr/intr)*	smell; sniff **45**
olfatear *(tr)*	sniff **2**
olvidar *(tr/intr)*	forget, leave behind, overlook **2**
omitir *(tr)*	leave out, omit **4**
ondular *(tr/intr)*	wave **2**
operar *(tr/intr)*	operate **2**
opinar *(tr/intr)*	have an opinion, have the opinion that, think of **2**
oponer(se) a *(tr/intr)*	oppose, stand out against **47**
optar por *(tr)*	decide on, opt for **2**
orar *(intr)*	pray **2**
orbitar *(tr/intr)*	orbit **2**
ordenar *(tr)*	command, order, put in order, sort **2**
ordeñar *(tr)*	milk **2**
organizar *(tr)*	organize **6**
orinar *(intr)*	urinate **2**
osar *(intr)*	dare **2**
oscilar (entre) *(Intr)*	range (*between*); oscillate, sway, swing **2**
oscurecer *(intr)*	darken; grow dark **32**
ostentar *(tr)*	show off; boast; hold a post **2**
otorgar *(tr)*	award (*prize*, etc.); confer, grant **7**
oxidar(se) *(tr/refl)*	oxidize, rust **2**
P **pacer** *(tr/intr)*	graze **32**
padecer *(tr/intr)*	suffer **32**
padecer hambre *(intr)*	starve
***pagar** *(tr/intr)*	pay **7**
pagar y marcharse	check out
palear *(tr)*	paddle (*boat*); shovel **2**
palidecer *(intr)*	turn pale **32**
palpar *(tr)*	feel, touch **2**
palpitar *(intr)*	beat, palpitate, pound **2**

peinar *(tr)*	comb **2**
pelar *(tr)*	peel, cut hair **2**
pelearse *(refl)*	argue, fight, quarrel **2**
pellizcar *(tr)*	pinch **5**
pender *(intr)*	hang **3**
penetrar *(tr)*	penetrate; see through **2**
*pensar *(tr/intr)*	think; intend **19**
pensar en *(tr)*	think of
pensionar *(tr)*	pension **2**
percibir *(tr)*	discern, perceive, sense **4**
perder *(tr/intr)*	lose **19**
perder el conocimiento *(intr)*	faint, pass out
perder el tiempo *(intr)*	loiter, lose time
perder la paciencia *(intr)*	lose one's temper
perderse *(refl)*	get lost, stray **19**
perdonar *(tr)*	forgive, let off, pardon, spare (*life*) **2**
perdurar *(Intr)*	remain unchanged **2**
perecer *(intr)*	perish **32**
perfeccionar(se) *(tr/refl)*	improve, perfect **2**
perfilar *(tr)*	outline **2**
perforar *(tr)*	perforate; drill; sink (*well*) **2**
perfumar *(tr)*	perfume, scent **2**
perjudicar *(tr)*	damage, harm **5**
permanecer *(intr)*	remain, stay **32**
permitir *(tr)*	allow, let, permit **4**
pernoctar *(intr)*	spend the night somewhere **2**
perpetuar *(tr)*	perpetuate **15**
perseguir *(tr/intr)*	chase, hound, pursue **10**
persistir *(intr)*	keep on, persist **4**
persuadir *(tr)*	persuade **4**
pertenecer *(intr)*	belong **32**
perturbar *(tr)*	disturb **2**
pesar *(tr/intr)*	weigh **2**
pescar *(tr)*	fish **5**
pestañear *(intr)*	blink **2**
picar *(tr)*	prick, sting, itch; mince (*food*); bite (*insect*) **5**
picotear *(tr/intr)*	peck **2**

pillar *(tr)*	pillage; seize; catch out **2**
pilotar *(tr)*	fly, pilot **2**
pinchar *(tr)*	prick **2**
pintar *(tr/intr)*	paint; depict **2**
pisar *(tr/intr)*	step, tread **2**
pisotear *(tr)*	trample, tread **2**
planchar *(tr)*	iron **2**
planear *(tr/intr)*	plan; glide **2**
planificar *(tr)*	plan **5**
plantar *(tr)*	plant **2**
platear *(tr)*	silver **2**
platicar *(intr)*	chat, talk **5**
plegar(se) *(tr/refl)*	fold, pleat; crease, wrinkle **7, 19**
plisar *(tr)*	pleat **2**
podar *(tr)*	prune **2**
*poder *(intr)*	be able to; can; may (*in requests*, etc.) **46**
polucionar *(tr)*	pollute **2**
polvorear *(tr)*	powder **2**
*poner *(tr)*	place, put; switch on **47**
poner a flotar *(tr)*	float
poner al revés *(tr)*	turn upside down
poner del revés *(tr)*	turn inside out
poner en libertad *(tr)*	free, set free
poner en obra *(tr)*	put into practice
poner en orden *(tr)*	put in order; tidy up
poner en una lista *(tr)*	list
poner guarniciones *(tr)*	harness
poner huevos *(intr)*	lay eggs
poner la mesa *(intr)*	set (*table*)
poner las esposas *(tr)*	handcuff
poner más fuerte *(tr)*	turn up (*volume*)
ponerse *(refl)*	become (e.g., *emotion*), turn (e.g., *angry*); dress in, put on **47**
ponerse de acuerdo	agree to
ponerse de pie	stand up
ponerse de pie de un salto	jump up
ponerse de rodillas	kneel down

ponerse en camino	set off, start, start out
ponerse enfermo	become ill
poner(se) moreno *(tr/refl)*	tan
ponerse nervioso	get worked up
portarse *(refl)*	behave **2**
poseer *(tr)*	own, possess, have **13**
posponer *(tr)*	postpone **47**
potenciar *(tr)*	potentiate **2**
practicar *(tr/intr)*	drill, practice **5**
precipitar(se) *(tr/refl)*	precipitate, rush, hasten **2**
precisar *(tr)*	pin (oneself) down **2**
predecir *(tr)*	predict **34**
predicar *(tr/intr)*	preach **5**
preferir *(tr)*	prefer **22**
preguntar *(tr)*	ask, Inquire, question **2**
preguntar por	ask for/after (*a person*)
preguntarse *(refl)*	ask oneself, wonder **2**
prender *(tr)*	capture, take **3**
prender con un alfiler *(tr)*	pin
preocupar(se) *(refl)*	worry **2**
preparar(se) *(tr/refl)*	get ready, prepare **2**
prescindir de *(tr)*	dispense with, do without **4**
presenciar *(tr)*	witness **2**
presentar *(tr)*	display, present, send in; show (e.g., *ticket*) **2**
presentarse a *(refl)*	apply (*for a job*); go in for, show up
preservar *(tr)*	preserve **2**
presidir *(tr/intr)*	chair, preside **4**
presionar *(tr)*	depress, press (*button*, etc.), push down **2**
prestar *(tr)*	lend **2**
prestar atención *(intr)*	pay attention
presupuestar *(tr)*	budget **2**
pretender *(tr)*	pretend; seek to **3**
prevenir *(tr)*	prevent, warn **57**
prever *(tr)*	forecast, foresee **58**
privar de *(tr)*	deprive, do out of **2**
privar de comida *(tr)*	starve

VERB INDEX

pulverizar(se) *(tr/refl)*	pulverize	**6**
purificar *(tr)*	purify, refine	**5**

Q

quebrar(se) *(tr/refl)*	break, smash	**19**
quedar *(intr)*	remain, stay	**2**
quedar en pie *(intr)*	remain standing, stand	
quedar en *(tr)*	decide on	
quedar sin *(tr)*	run out of	
quedar(se) *(refl)*	stay, remain, stay behind	**2**
quedarse atrás	drop behind	
quedarse dormido *(intr)*	fall asleep, nod off	
quejar(se) *(intr/refl)*	complain, groan, grumble, moan	**2**
*querer *(tr)*	want; wish; love	**48**
querer *(+ infinitive)*	want to do something	
querer decir *(tr)*	mean	
quitar(se) *(tr/refl)*	take off; clear away; withdraw; remove, take away	**2**
quitar el polvo *(tr)*	dust	

R

racionar *(tr)*	ration	**2**
radiografiar *(tr)*	X-ray	**14**
raer *(tr)*	scrape	**30**
rajar(se) *(tr/refl)*	crack, split; expel	**2**
rallar *(tr)*	grate	**2**
raptar *(tr)*	kidnap	**2**
rascar(se) *(tr/refl)*	scratch	**5**
rasgar(se) *(tr/refl)*	tear	**7**
rasguñar *(tr/intr)*	scratch	**2**
raspar *(tr)*	scrape	**2**
rastrear *(tr)*	track, trail	**2**
rastrillar *(tr)*	rake	**2**
ratificar *(tr)*	endorse, ratify	**5**
rayar *(tr)*	rule *(paper)*	**2**
razonar *(intr)*	reason	**2**
reaccionar *(tr)*	react	**2**
realizar *(tr)*	carry out, perform; fulfill, make real, realize; achieve, complete	**6**

VERB INDEX

reducir la velocidad *(tr/intr)*	slow down
reducir progresivamente *(tr)*	phase out
reembolsar *(tr)*	refund, reimburse 2
reemplazar *(tr)*	replace 6
referirse a *(refl)*	refer to 22
refinar *(tr)*	refine 2
reflejar *(tr)*	reflect 2
reflexionar *(intr)*	reflect, think over 2
reforzar *(tr)*	reinforce, strengthen 6, 20
refrenar *(tr)*	restrain, stem 2
refrescar(se) *(tr/refl)*	freshen, refresh 5
refrigerar *(tr)*	refrigerate 2
refunfuñar *(intr)*	grumble 2
refutar *(tr)*	refute 2
regalar *(tr)*	give away *(as a present)* 2
regañar *(tr)*	nag, scold 2
regar *(tr)*	irrigate, spray, water *(plants)* 7, 19
regatear *(intr)*	bargain, haggle 2
regontar *(tr)*	boss about 2
regir *(tr)*	govern, rule 11, 24
registrar *(tr)*	register, record, enroll; look through, scan 2
registrarse *(refl)*	register *(in a hotel)*
reglamentar *(intr)*	make regulations, regulate 2
regocijar(se) *(tr/refl)*	rejoice 2
regresar *(intr)*	come/go home/back, get back, return 2
regular *(tr)*	regulate 2
regularizar *(tr)*	standardize 6
rehacer *(tr)*	redo; remake 41
rehusar *(intr)*	refuse 2
reinar *(intr)*	reigns, rule 2
reintegrar *(tr)*	refund 2
reiterar *(tr)*	reiterate 2
*reír(se) *(refl)*	laugh 49
relacionar *(tr)*	relate 2
relajar *(tr/intr)*	relax 2
relampaguear *(intr)*	flash (lightning) 2

relatar *(tr)*	report, tell	**2**
relinchar *(intr)*	neigh	**2**
rellenar *(tr)*	fill, stuff	**2**
relucir *(intr)*	gleam, shine	**43**
remar *(intr)*	row *(boat)*	**2**
rematar *(tr)*	crown, finish off, finishing touches to	**2**
remendar *(tr)*	patch	**19**
remojar(se) *(tr/refl)*	soak, steep	**2**
remolcar *(tr)*	tow	**5**
remontar a *(intr)*	date back to	**2**
remontarse *(refl)*	soar	**2**
remover *(tr)*	stir	**20**
rendir(se) *(tr/refl)*	produce, yield; capitulate, give up, surrender	**24**
renovar(se) *(tr/refl)*	renew, renovate	**20**
renunciar *(tr)*	disclaim, give up, renounce, resign	**2**
reñir *(intr)*	argue, quarrel	**17, 24**
reorganizar(se) *(tr/refl)*	reorganize	**6**
reparar *(tr)*	fix, repair	**2**
repartir *(tr)*	distribute, give out, hand out, share out	**4**
repasar *(tr)*	revise, study again	**2**
repetir *(tr)*	repeat; play back	**24**
repicar *(intr)*	chime, peal	**5**
reponerse *(refl)*	get fit, recover *(health)*	**47**
represar *(tr)*	dam, repress	**2**
representar *(tr/intr)*	represent; depict, perform, play a role, portray, stage; show, put on *(play)*, stand for	**2**
reprochar *(tr)*	reproach	**2**
reproducir(se) *(tr/refl)*	reproduce	**31**
repugnar *(tr)*	disgust	**2**
requerir *(tr)*	require; call for, summon; want demand	**22**
resbalar *(intr)*	skid, slide, slip	**2**
rescatar *(tr)*	rescue	**2**
reservar *(tr)*	reserve	**2**

resistir *(intr)*	resist, stand up to; endure, hold out **4**
resollar *(intr)*	pant **2**
resolver *(tr)*	resolve, solve, figure/work out *(solution)* **20**
resolver(se) a *(tr/refl)*	make up one's mind, resolve (to) **20**
resonar *(intr)*	blare, resound, sound **20**
respaldar *(tr)*	support **2**
respetar *(tr)*	respect **2**
respirar *(intr)*	breathe **2**
respirar con dificultad *(intr)*	gasp
responder *(tr)*	reply **3**
responder de *(tr)*	account for
restar *(tr)*	subtract **2**
restaurar *(tr)*	restore **2**
restregar *(tr)*	rub, scrub **7**
restringir *(tr)*	limit, restrict **11**
resucitar *(tr/intr)*	revive **2**
resultar *(intr)*	result, turn out, work out **2**
resumir *(tr)*	summarize, sum up **4**
retar *(tr)*	challenge **2**
retardar *(tr)*	delay, slow down **2**
retener *(tr)*	hold back, keep back, retain **54**
retirar(se) *(tr/refl)*	retire; cancel; take out, withdraw *(money from bank*, etc.) **2**
retorcer(se) *(tr/refl)*	twist **9**
retransmitir *(tr)*	relay **4**
retrasar *(tr)*	delay **2**
retroceder *(intr)*	stand back, turn back **3**
retumbar *(intr)*	resound, rumble **2**
reunir(se) *(tr/refl)*	join, reunite, rejoin; collect, gather, meet **15**
revelar *(tr)*	disclose, reveal, show **2**
reventar *(intr)*	burst, explode **19**
revestir *(tr)*	coat, cover **24**
revestir de acero *(tr)*	cover with steel
revestir de hormigón *(tr)*	cover with concrete
revisar *(tr)*	check, check over, revise **2**

revisar cuentas	audit
revolotear *(intr)*	fly about, wheel **2**
revolver *(intr)*	turn around **20**
rezar *(intr)*	pray **6**
ridiculizar *(tr)*	ridicule **6**
rizar *(tr)*	curl **6**
robar *(tr)*	burglarize/burgle, rob, steal **2**
rociar *(tr)*	spatter, sprinkle **14**
rodar *(intr)*	bowl; roll, wheel; shoot (*film*) **20**
rodear *(tr)*	circle, close in, encircle, skirt, surround **2**
roer *(tr)*	gnaw **30**
rogar *(tr)*	beg, plead, pray, request **7, 20**
***romper(se)** *(tr/refl)*	break **50**
roncar *(intr)*	snore **5**
ronronear *(intr)*	purr **2**
rozar *(tr)*	brush against **6**
ruborizarse *(refl)*	blush **6**
rugir *(intr)*	roar **11**

S

***saber** *(tr/intr)*	know; know how to; learn **51**
saborear *(tr)*	savor **2**
***sacar** *(tr)*	take out, get out, withdraw; stick out; draw **5**
sacar con cuchara *(tr)*	scoop
sacar de quicio *(tr)*	irritate, madden
sacar ganancia (de) *(intr)*	benefit, profit (from)
sacar una foto *(tr)*	take a photograph
saciar *(tr)*	quench **2**
sacrificar *(tr)*	sacrifice **5**
sacudir(se) *(tr/refl)*	rock, shake **4**
salar *(tr)*	salt **2**
saldar *(tr)*	pay off **2**
***salir** *(intr)*	get/go/come out; exit, leave, depart; branch off; rise (*sun, moon*) **52**
salir a escena *(intr)*	come on (stage)
salir bien *(intr)*	come out well, succeed
salir mal *(intr)*	turn out badly

salir como un huracán	storm out
salir del huevo *(intr)*	hatch out
salir violentamente *(intr)*	burst out
salpicar *(tr)*	scatter, spatter, splash, sprinkle **5**
saltar *(intr)*	jump, leap, spring **2**
saludar *(tr)*	greet **2**
salvar *(tr)*	salvage, save **2**
sanar *(tr/intr)*	heal **2**
sangrar *(intr)*	bleed **2**
satisfacer *(tr)*	satisfy **41**
sazonar *(tr)*	season **2**
secar(se) *(tr/refl)*	wipe, dry, dry out **5**
secuestrar *(tr)*	hijack, kidnap **2**
seducir *(tr)*	lure, seduce **31**
segar *(tr)*	mow, reap **7**
seguir *(tr/intr)*	continue, go on; keep (on) . . . ing; come after, follow **10, 24**
seguir fiel a *(intr)*	stick to
seleccionar *(tr)*	choose, pick, select **2**
sellar *(tr)*	seal **2**
sembrar *(tr)*	plant, sow **19**
señalar *(tr)*	indicate, point (out/to); sign, signal **2**
sentar(se) *(tr/refl)*	sit, seat (someone else); suit **19**
sentarse a la mesa *(refl)*	sit at table
sentenciar *(tr)*	sentence **2**
***sentir** *(tr/intr)*	feel, sense; be sorry, regret **22**
separar(se) de *(tr/refl)*	break off, separate, spread out **2**
sepultar *(tr)*	bury **2**
***ser** *(intr)*	be **53**
ser cuestión de *(intr)*	be a matter of
ser diferente de	be different from
ser escritor *(intr)*	be a writer (*career*)
ser una estrella *(intr)*	star
ser miembro de	be a member of
ser necesario	be necessary

ser operado	have an operation
ser paciente	be patient
ser permitido	be allowed
ser responsable de	be liable for, be responsible for
ser socio de	be a member of
ser valedero	be valid
serrar *(tr)*	saw **19**
servir *(tr)*	serve **24**
servir a alguien *(tr)*	wait on someone
servir para *(intr)*	to be useful for
servirse *(refl)*	help oneself **24**
servirse de *(refl)*	make use of
sesgar *(tr)*	put skew, slant **7**
significar *(tr)*	denote, mean, signify **5**
silbar *(intr)*	whistle; hiss **2**
simular *(tr)*	pretend **2**
sintetizar *(tr)*	synthesize **6**
sintonizar *(intr)*	tune in **6**
sisar *(tr)*	steal, swipe **2**
sisear *(intr)*	hiss **2**
sitiar *(tr)*	besiege **2**
situar *(tr)*	place, site, situate **15**
sobornar *(tr)*	bribe **2**
sobrepasar *(tr)*	surpass **2**
sobresalir *(intr)*	jut out, overhang; stand out; bulge **52**
sobresaltar(se) *(tr/refl)*	alarm, frighten, shock, start, startle **2**
sobrevivir *(intr)*	survive **4**
sofocar(se) *(tr/refl)*	choke, suffocate **5**
soldar(se) *(tr/refl)*	weld **20**
soler *(tr)*	be accustomed to **20**
solicitar *(tr)*	beg for, request **2**
solidificar(se) *(tr/refl)*	solidify **5**
sollozar *(intr)*	sob **6**
soltar *(tr)*	let go, release; cast off (*boat*); loosen **20**
solucionar *(tr)*	solve **2**
sombrear *(tr)*	shade **2**

someter(se) *(tr/refl)*	submit, subject; yield **3**
sonar *(tr/intr)*	sound **20**
soñar *(tr/intr)*	dream **20**
soñar despierto *(intr)*	daydream
sonreír *(intr)*	smile **49**
sonrojarse *(refl)*	blush **2**
soplar *(intr)*	blow **2**
soportar *(tr)*	bear, endure, stand, support **2**
sorber *(tr)*	sip **3**
sorprender *(tr)*	catch out, surprise **3**
sosegar *(tr)*	calm **7, 19**
sospechar *(tr)*	suspect **2**
sostener *(tr)*	hold up, support, sustain **54**
subir *(intr)*	climb, get on, increase (*prices*), go up; como in (*tide*), rise (e g., *slope*) **4**
subir (a) *(tr)*	increase, lift, raise; board, climb **4**
sublevarse *(refl)*	rebel **2**
subrayar *(tr)*	emphasize, highlight, stress, underline **2**
subsidiar *(tr)*	subsidize **2**
subvencionar *(tr)*	subsidize **2**
suceder *(intr)*	happen, occur; follow, succeed **3**
sudar *(intr)*	sweat **2**
sufrir *(tr/intr)*	suffer, undergo **4**
sugerir *(tr)*	suggest **22**
sujetar *(tr)*	attach, fasten, fix; clamp, hold down **2**
sujetar con un peso *(tr)*	weigh down
sumar *(tr/intr)*	add, amount, number **2**
sumergir(se) *(tr/refl/intr)*	immerse, plunge, submerge **11**
suministrar *(tr)*	furnish, provide, supply **2**
superar *(tr)*	overcome, surpass **2**
supervisar *(tr)*	supervise **2**
suplicar *(tr)*	beg, pray **5**
suplir *(intr)*	stand in for, substitute **4**
suponer *(tr)*	suppose **47**

suprimir *(tr)*	abolish, excise, suppress **4**
surgir *(intr)*	arise (e.g., *problem*) **11**
surtir *(tr)*	stock, supply **4**
suscribir *(intr)*	subscribe **37**
suspender *(tr)*	suspend, call off; give a failing grade **3**
suspirar *(intr)*	sigh **2**
suspirar por *(intr)*	pine for
sustituir *(tr)*	change, replace, substitute **12**
sustraer *(tr)*	subtract **55**
susurrar *(intr)*	whisper **2**

T

tachar *(tr)*	cross out, delete, erase **2**
tajar *(tr)*	chop, cut, hack, slice **2**
taladrar *(tr)*	drill **2**
tallar *(tr)*	hew **2**
tambalear(se) *(intr/refl)*	stagger, totter **2**
tamborilear *(intr)*	drum/patter **2**
tamizar *(tr)*	screen, sieve, sift **6**
tañer *(tr)*	pluck, play (*instrument*) **17**
tapar *(tr)*	block, plug **2**
taponar *(tr)*	cork **2**
tardar *(intr)*	delay, linger **2**
tartamudear *(intr)*	stammer, stutter **2**
tasar *(tr)*	appraise, price **2**
techar *(tr)*	put a roof on **2**
tejer *(tr/intr)*	spin (*wool*), weave **3**
telefonear *(tr)*	call, (tele)phone **2**
temblar *(intr)*	quiver, shiver, tremble **19**
temer *(tr)*	dread, fear **3**
templar *(tr)*	moderate, temper **2**
tender(se) *(tr/refl)*	lie, spread, stretch out **19**
tender a *(intr)*	tend, be likely to
tender una embuscada *(intr)*	ambush
*tener *(tr)*	have; hold **54**
tener aversión a *(tr)*	dislike
tener cariño a *(tr)*	have affection for
tener cuidado *(intr)*	look out, take care

tener en cuenta *(tr)*	consider
tener en mente *(tr)*	have in mind
tener éxito *(intr)*	succeed
tener frío	be cold
tener diarrea	have diarrhea
tener lástima a/de *(tr)*	pity, take pity on
tener lugar *(intr)*	take place
tener miedo (a) *(tr/intr)*	be afraid, be frightened, fear
tener que *(intr)*	have to, must
tener que ver con *(tr)*	concern
tener razón	be right
tener sabor a *(intr)*	taste like
tener un accidente *(intr)*	have an accident
tensar *(tr)*	tense **2**
tentar *(tr)*	feel; explore; attempt; entice, lure, tempt **19**
teñir *(tr)*	dye, stain **17, 24**
terminar(se) *(tr/intr/refl)*	complete, end, end up, finish, stop **2**
tirar *(tr/intr)*	draw, haul, heave, pull, tow; shoot, fire; bowl, throw **2**
tirarse al agua *(refl)*	dive
titubear *(intr)*	stagger; hesitate **5**
tocar *(tr)*	pat, touch, play *(musical instrument)* **5**
tocar el tambor *(tr)*	drum
tolerar *(tr)*	bear, endure stand *(put up with)*, tolerate
tomar *(tr)*	take *(eat or drink)*, have **2**
tomar en cuenta *(tr)*	take into account
tomar nota	take note
tomar parte *(intr)*	take part
tomarse la molestia	take trouble
topar *(tr)*	bump into, come across, run into **2**
torcer(se) *(tr/refl)*	bend *(road)*, turn, twist; pull a muscle, sprain; curve; screw **9, 20**
torturar *(tr)*	torture **2**